MW00927717

deciding

clarifying your kingdom contribution

AS INTRODUCED IN THE BOOK *STUCK!*

TERRY B. WALLING

w/ Rick Williams & Steve Hopkins

© 2017 Terry Walling

Leader Breakthru
Resourcing and coaching breakthrough
in the lives of risk-taking, Kingdom leaders.

www.leaderbreakthru.com

Unless otherwise noted, all biblical quotations come from THE HOLY BIBLE,
NEW INTERNATIONAL VERSION®, NIV® Copyright © 1973, 1978, 1984,
2011 by Biblica, Inc.® Used by permission. All rights reserved worldwide.

*Like the woman at the well, sooner or later,
perhaps in a quiet, reflective moment, we must
all come to terms with the honest truth that we were
looking for more than we've found thus far.*[1]

—M. CRAIG BARNES

contents

before words: *Terry*

Deciding has not been an easy book to write. There are reasons for that.

Besides the normal challenges of putting thoughts into print and wanting those insights to be helpful to others, the topic of *contribution* draws resistance. While I do not see a devil under every rock, after thirty years of coaching individuals who want to see their lives count for Christ, the enemy does not want issues of Kingdom contribution to be clarified.

Calling begins a journey of purpose, but contribution moves calling beyond our initial commitment to follow Christ and into active decision-making related to making a difference for Christ. That draws enemy fire. We lose many well meaning Christ-followers as they grapple with the issues that surround contribution. We accept our calling, but we must embrace our contribution.

Deciding helps to catalyze the choices that surround the second half of our journey as a Christ-follower. Christ himself made many choices as He lived out his call and mission, including the day He set his face toward Jerusalem (Luke 9:51) and the cross. We too must make choices that are required to move beyond the demands of the crowd, and into lives that align with His purposes. Many times these choices will mean saying *NO* to good things in order to say *YES* to what's best.

Deciding is also a call for you to go deeper in your walk with Christ. What got you to this point in your journey with Christ may not take you to a new place in your personal intimacy with Christ. In order for your influence to go wider, Christ must take you deeper. (Galatians 4:19).

The Father has designed a plan, the Son has modeled the course, and the Spirit stands ready to guide you into all truth, but the choices ahead are yours.

Terry Walling
January 2018

before words: *Rick*

As iron sharpens iron, so one person sharpens another. —Proverbs 27:17

You don't get to clarity alone.
—Terry Walling

The truths you will read in the pages ahead helped me at an important moment in my journey. I have discovered the incredible value of being sharpened and shaped by those who have been down the same roads before me.

When I decided to run a marathon in 2007, and celebrate my 50th birthday, my first thought was I need a coach. God provided a coach for me. Every Saturday morning, Lou would run alongside me. He did this for my 16-week training schedule. I would ask all kinds of questions of this 67-year-old man. I would ask questions about my running shoes, running pace, proper hydration, and many other marathon-related questions. I listened attentively to Lou. Why? Because Lou had run many half marathons, full marathons even triathlons. He knew what I would be facing. He knew what was ahead.

There is a far more important race you and I are running. It is a spiritual race marked out for each of us by God (Hebrews 12:2). We need a coach for this spiritual race if we are going to finish well. God has used the insights of this book and Terry to help me navigate the various transitions of my journey. I am grateful for his friendship, mentoring, and coaching during my Deciding Transition.

It has been a privilege to contribute to this book. My hope and desire is that God will use my story to help inform your story. I have found it to be true that each of us needs to see "a" way before we can find "our" way. Hopefully you will find your way through the Deciding Transition as you read my story and interact with this book.

Rick Williams
November 2017

before words: *Steve*

Many years ago the Father taught me that's what important is not how many people hear my voice, *but how many people hear His voice.* Those I have the opportunity to serve and help need to hear His words much more than they need to hear mine. As I acknowledge my total dependence on the Lord and surrender to Him, I then must adopt a posture of listening to Him. My wife needs a husband, my family needs a father, father-in-law, and papaw who is listening to the Father. Leaders and Christ-followers alike need to be able to hear *His voice,* over our own.

The most important prayer each of us can pray is: *"God, be merciful to me, a sinner."* (Luke 18:13) The second most important prayer is: *"Speak Lord, Your servant is listening."* (1 Samuel 3:9-10).

Writing my chapter for *Deciding* challenged me to listen to the Father in greater ways—listening for His voice and His word for you. Like Paul, I share *"in weakness, in fear, and in much trembling,"* trusting the Spirit to *"explain spiritual things to spiritual people."* (1 Corinthians 2:3, 13) Be like those in Berea who *"received the word with eagerness and examined the Scriptures daily to see if these things were so."* (Acts 17:11)

If you find yourself in the Deciding Transition—ask the Father to reveal the insights you need, and make sure you find a coach who can walk with you. Terry often reminds me that we don't get to clarity alone. Coaching and opportunities to facilitate help leaders remove the barriers we often have to hearing His voice. There are times we all need a *Priscilla and Aquila* that help us take the next steps of faith (Acts 18:24-28) Look for someone who will point you to Jesus, and allow Him to be the Hero. As you help others, be one who has a *"God-listening heart"* that you might lead His people well. (1 Kings 3:9 MSG)

Steve Hopkins
November 2017

thanks & dedications

The authors wish to thank the many who have helped with the creation of this new resource. First and foremost, thanks go out to all the leaders whose lives, coaching and openness to the Spirit of God helped surface these insights and frame the issues found within these pages. Their breakthroughs became our discoveries.

We greatly thank *Dr. J. Robert Clinton* for his research and insights related to lifelong formation and leadership development. His work of more than forty years and his classes at Fuller Seminary provide the foundational base for this work.

We thank *Sue Grant and Denise Hopkins* for their work in the reading and editing of the manuscript.

We thank *Kyle and Megan Walling* for their graphic design work related to all three books in this series, and for their help editing and formatting this book to make these insights more accessible.

We thank the *Leader Breakthru Hub Leaders, along with our colleagues, coaches and facilitators.* Each play an important part in Leader Breakthru, providing continued insights and clarity in these concepts.

Terry wishes to thank and dedicate this resource to:
Blaine and Doris Walling, my parents, whose lives lived for Christ, and their love for the Church, shaped my life and its contribution.

Rick thanks and dedicates this resource to:
Lisa, my wife and soul mate whom God has used to encourage me, and model for me the joy of Jesus!

Steve thanks and dedicates this resource to:
Denise, a gift from the Father, we get to live the miracle of marriage every day, two becoming one—awesome!

getting the most out of *deciding*

Deciding is a different kind of book.

Most books seek to introduce new concepts, ideas and paradigms, hoping to demonstrate their relevance and convince you of their validity. *Deciding* was written for the convinced. It is for those in the mid-stage of life who know about the frustration of living in the in-between. Their sense is that God is at work doing something new, but they have little or no insight into what that might be, or what may lie ahead. This paralyzing moment is called the Deciding Transition, and it occurs for all Christ-followers somewhere in the early 40s to late 50s. The Deciding Transition begins to clarify a Christ-follower's unique Kingdom contribution. Contribution seeks to define the influence and role we each play in the lives of those we touch and in the places we serve.

God does some of His greatest shaping work during times of transition. Transitions serve to catalyze new direction, clarify values, provide insight for decision-making, and bring closure to the past. Though most of us want out of a time of transition, God wants in. The question is not whether we will enter in to times of transition, but rather will we be patiently present, getting out all that God has for us during that time.

Deciding is based on forty years of research related to lifelong development from *Dr. J. Robert Clinton* (former Professor of Leadership Development at Fuller Seminary) and thirty years of personal development coaching by *Dr. Terry Walling* of Leader Breakthru. The insights found in these pages will better acquaint you with the nature of transitions, and will guide you as you process your Deciding Transition. Staying the course during a transition is no easy feat. Transitions are often more about perseverance than immediate insight.

Below are three tips that can help you get the most out of your time of transition, as well as how to get the most out of *Deciding*.

First, read *Deciding* as an overall interpretive guide. The core purpose of this resource is to help provide you with definitions, labels and insights related to the journey through the Deciding Transition. Not all Deciding Transitions will include everything you will read about in this book, but the words ahead can provide both reassurance and hope in knowing that you are not lost, and that what you are experiencing is not unique only to you. We have found that the more labels and language you can gain related to a transition, the better able you will be to navigate the uncertain waters in you are in.

Second, utilize *Deciding* as an interactive map that can be explored with others. Use this book as a small group discussion resource, or as a companion to personal coaching. Discovery happens best in community. A small group format guide, and coaching questions have been provided in the Appendix.

Third, allow *Deciding* to act as a compass to help you track where you are during your time of transition. Transitions take time, and can last from three months to three years. Sit with these concepts, then begin to live them out, being sure to revisit to them over time. Give God room and time to work. A good rule of thumb for decision-making during a time of transition, as much as it is up to you, only make *lasting decisions* once you navigated the last of your transition. That is, when possible, hold off on making major decisions until you have gained all that you can out of your transition.

Three voices will offer their insights related to the Deciding Transition.

Terry Walling, author of *Stuck!* and founder of Leader Breakthru, serves as your core guide through the Deciding Transition. Terry coaches and resources the personal development of leaders, and knows these waters well. He will share insights and issues along the way related to lifelong formation and leadership development. Terry coaches Rick Williams throughout the book, and provides greater understanding of the Deciding Transition in the "Back Story" sections in chapters 4-8.

Rick Williams is Senior pastor of a local church and shares his actual journey as he experienced the Deciding Transition. The narrative of his transition is found in chapters 4-8. Rick offers you an inside look into his transition as a case study and shares a journal of his thoughts and emotions related to the process.

Note that the narrative of Rick's transition has been adapted to fit the format of the book, but the issues discussed are the same ones that occurred as his Deciding Transition progressed.

Steve Hopkins offers his unique experience as one who has utilized these concepts while serving as a Director of Leadership Development for a State Convention of the Southern Baptist Church in Ohio. Steve trains leaders and equips pastors to better understand issues of calling and contribution. In chapter 10, Steve helps address obstacles, road-blocks and challenges that he has observed as individuals have worked through the Deciding Transition. Steve focuses on how the mid-game of a Christ-follower's life often presents a "Danger Zone" for many as they seek to move forward in their development as believers.

The Deciding Transition was first introduced in the book: *Stuck! Navigating the Transitions of Life and Leadership*, by Terry Walling. *Stuck!* helps to define transitions and explain how God uses transitions to develop His disciples. After the release of *Stuck!*, individuals voiced a desire for more help navigating each of the three transitions introduced in *Stuck!*. Three books have now been developed, one on each of the three transitions; *Awakening*, *Deciding* and *Finishing*. Each transition, and its resources, are featured on the Leader Breakthru website (leaderbreakthru.com).

Deciding has been organized into four-parts:

Part One consists of three chapters that define the Deciding Transition and provide an overview of the issues related to contribution. Each chapter builds a foundational understanding of contribution and what to expect as the Deciding Transition progresses.

Part Two shares Rick Williams' Deciding Transition in narrative form, chronicling the coaching appointments that transpired between Rick and Terry. Chapters 4-8, and Rick's coaching appointments follow the *Transition Life Cycle* (see fig. 1 on page 17). Each chapter includes: (1) the coaching narrative, (2) the "Back Story," which provides personal development content to help interpret what is occurring, and (3) "Rick's Journal Entry" highlighting his thoughts and emotions as he processed his transition.

Part Three provides interpretive help related to issues and obstacles that the Deciding Transition often presents.

In chapter 9, Rick shares four postures (or commitments) which allowed him to stay the course, and get all he could out of his transition. The four postures Rick utilized are: renewal, solitude, self-care, and coaching.

In chapter 10, Steve introduces common traps that can derail a Christ-follower as they seek to navigate the Deciding Transition. He also describes the "Danger Zone" and what can occur when behavior patterns create a plateau even in the most well-meaning believers.

In chapter 11, Terry discusses *differentiation* and how God uses the Deciding Transition to surface issues of self-awareness. Greater clarity and acceptance of one's God-given identity is an important part of the process of discovering one's unique, Kingdom contribution.

Part Four highlights additional resources from Leader Breakthru that can help an individual navigate the Deciding Transition. It also includes a message to leaders and pastors.

Chapter 12 provides a summary of Leader Breakthru's Apex Process, which is designed to help Christ-followers discover their unique, Kingdom contribution.

Chapter 13 was written specifically for leaders and pastors who are in vocational ministry. In particular, it raises issues related to spiritual authority during the Deciding Transition. Often times, God uses this transition to take leaders to a new level of influence and spiritual authority, moving them beyond relying on their natural abilities alone.

The Appendices offer a Small Group Guide and coaching questions for those who seek to process this transition with others.

THE IMPORTANCE OF COACHING

We do not get to clarity alone.

Coaching is essential for processing any transition.

Many organizations offer coaching and access to trained coaches. Leader Breakthru offers coaches and coach training that specialize in personal development life coaching. Contact Leader Breakthru to find a coach, or to attend our training events (leaderbreakthru.com/contact).

Note: A Coaching Guide and coaching questions have been provided in Appendix B. of this book, along with a Small Group Discussion guide (Appendix A.). These can be used in a group-coaching experience.

THE AUTHOR AND FINISHER

The Deciding Transition is an important crossroads moment in the development of a Christ-follower. It is important to know that He who began this new work in your life is still at work, and will be faithful to complete it. Jesus Christ is the author and finisher of our faith (Philippians 1:6). He shapes our lives utilizing the people, events and circumstances. The twists and turns in our development are never outside his privy or design. The prize of surrendering to His work is greater revelation in understanding His work. The more we align, the more we are able to recognize His sovereign design.

The days ahead hold strategic keys for your future.

Transitions provide windows into God's shaping work. Approach your transition with a sovereign mindset.

summary: *the deciding transition*

Transitions are like 'eddies' that occur within the flow of a river. Eddies form on the side of a river, typically after a turn in the water flow, or behind a boulder that is wedged in the river. The water flow in an eddy gives the appearance of a whirlpool, circular in motion, making its own path as it flows with and against the direction of the rest of the river. Its swirling motion can often be violent or slow. It can appear chaotic or methodical in nature. Imagine driftwood caught in that flow. As it progresses around, often times within the swirl of the water, the mass of materials eventually works its way back out, released from the control of the circular current, and back into the mainstream of the river.

William Bridges, author of the book, *Transitions* notes that at their core, transitions are typically comprised of: "(1) an ending, followed by (2) a period of confusion and distress, leading to (3) a new beginning. Bridges goes on to say: "those who have gone into a transition unwillingly or unwittingly find it hard to admit that a new beginning and a new phase of their lives might be at hand."[2]

Transitions typically have a life of their own. Each phase of a transition seeks to lead an individual to the new place God desires for them. The four phases of a transition are pictured in *The Transition Life Cycle* (see fig. 1 on page 17).

"There are three important transitions that occur in the personal development of committed and passionate Christ-followers. These major transitions move one toward greater influence and growth, helping to shape a life for a unique and ultimate contribution, whether one works and ministers in a vocational ministry role or lives and serves Christ in the marketplace."[3]

These three major transitions are:

- The Awakening Transition (often occurring in one's 20s or 30s)

- The Deciding Transition (often occurring in one's 40s or 50s)

- The Finishing Transition (often occurring one's 60s or 70s)

Common characteristics of all transition moments include:

- Continued sense of restlessness
- Prolonged confusion
- New or resurfacing of self-doubt
- Ongoing lack of motivation
- Sense of paralysis and prolonged inactivity
- Continuing uncertainty
- Diminished confidence
- Continued lack of clarity

Unique characteristics of the Deciding Transition include:

- Indecision related to gifting and abilities
- Uncertainty related to role on teams and contribution
- Questions related to generalist v. specialist
- Struggles with confidence and differentiation
- Problems with decision-making in terms of vocational direction
- Lack of fulfillment with one's current job
- Sustained lack of motivation and disbelief that one can find meaningful vocation

Essentials of the Deciding Transition

- Typical age range in which it occurs: 40s-50s
- Core Issue: *Life priorities*
- Core Topic: *An individual's contribution to others*
- Development Issue: *Differentiation*
- Practical Issue: *Understanding of one's role and influence*
- Behavioral Choices: *Decision-making grid to say yes and no*
- Internal Struggle: *Generalist vs. Unique contribution*
- What's at Stake: *Plateau in one's growth and development*

- What Not-to-Do (helpers): *Solve the issues or make decisions for them—robs ownership*

- Help Needed: *Processing, encouragement and challenge*

A FINAL NOTE:

Transitions take time. Transitions typically take anywhere from three months to three years. Transitions yield insights that will be needed in the future.

The most important thing is to get all you can out of a transition.

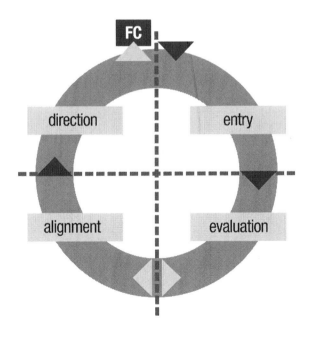

figure 1—The Transition Life Cycle

PART ONE

preparing

We look for the big things to do—Jesus took a towel and washed the disciples' feet. We presume the place to be is the mountaintop of vision— he sends us back into the valley. We like to speak and act out of the rare moments of inspiration—he requires our obedience in the routine, the unseen, and the thankless.[4]

—OS GUINNESS

We cannot escape most of the crises in our lives, nor should we. In fact, these events frequently provide the energy for movement on our spiritual journey, even when we are stuck along the way.[5]

—JANET HABGERG

WHAT'S AHEAD?

Important foundations need to be laid before we can go deeper in explaining and exploring the Deciding Transition. The core insight of Part One is how to distinguish the difference between *calling* and *contribution*.

Chapter One—*Beyond Calling* seeks to define and describe the second stage of a Christ-follower's development, moving them beyond understanding life's purpose, to making their unique contribution.

Chapter Two—*Choices* reveals that one of the core purposes of the Deciding Transition is to bring the Christ-follower face-to-face with the need for choices.

Chapter Three—*The Climb* will help review some of the major challenges faced as one seeks to clarify their contribution and influence.

1

beyond calling

Never once did it occur to me that when I found the trail again, it would ruin my life forever. For once you feel the breath of God breathe on your skin, you can never turn back, you can never settle for what was, you can only move on recklessly, with abandon, your heart filled with fear and your ears ringing with the constant words of encouragement, "Fear not!"[6]

—MIKE YACCONELLI

The more we get what we now call 'ourselves' out of the way and let Him take us over, the more truly ourselves we become.[7]

—C.S. LEWIS

SOMETHING MORE

Many Christ-followers are quietly leaving the church.

They remain passionate about Christ, and they hunger for a deeper journey with God, but they no longer see the local church as the place where they can go further in their walks with God. They are not mad, rather they have just grown uninterested. "Their leaving reflects first-hand experiences that have led them to conclude that churches are ill-equipped to support the life they hoped."[8] They are disengaging from the Church, but not from God.

In the past, those leaving have often been the disgruntled ones who wanted the ministries and the decisions of the church to fit *their* preferences. But many who leave now are ones who have led ministries, taught Bible studies and even served on church boards. They are the ones their local churches counted on to be there when the doors opened, but now many have gone missing. For all intent and purposes, they have become refugees, displaced by a church that decided to cater to those who were at the early stages of faith. Some have given this group a name: they are called the "dones," or the "dechurched."[9]

The research commissioned by Willow Creek Community Church in 2008, and its corresponding report entitled "*Reveal*," captured a startling truth:

> *Willow Creek had been successful in meeting the spiritual needs of those who described themselves as "exploring Christianity" or "growing in Christ," but it has been less successful at doing so with those who self-report as being "close to Christ" or "Christ-centered." In fact, one-fourth of the last two groups say that they are either "stalled" in their spiritual growth and/or dissatisfied with the church.*[10]

In recent years local churches (in the West) have spent much time and energy attracting seekers to its doors. Attempts have also been made to see those new attendees move toward "making a decision for Christ," and find their way into discipleship classes and small groups with the hope that their new faith in Christ would grow.

The church has gone even further.

Local churches have sought to communicate to responders and

seekers alike that they could live a life of purpose. Thousands have studied the purpose-driven life and learned that their life in Christ has meaning, beyond conversion. In small groups all over America, they heard that they are "called" by God to make a difference in their world. And yet, somehow and someway, these efforts did not translate into a deeper walk and life with Christ.

Could it be that there is something more?

It is interesting to note that there was <u>never</u> a time when Jesus stopped discipling the disciples. Every moment was used to shape their lives. And after He left, the discipling process continued. As the early church grew, their new assignments and tasks shaped their influence and called them into even deeper intimacy with Him.

The problem today is that many believers have been abandoned after the initial stages of the faith, leaving them unsure about what is next. The issue has not so much been the message or the messengers, but the approach. The expedient culture of our day has turned discipleship into 8-12 training sessions, held in a classroom, utilizing a "one-size-fits-all" framework. We have opted-out of Jesus' life-on-life approach. Jesus mentored and discipled according to the development of the individual (i.e., Peter was discipled differently than John, and different, still, from James) How to individualize each disciple's development today, while seeking to minister to large numbers of attenders is a significant challenge for the today's church.

Lifelong discipleship and leadership development is about the formation of the Christ-like life, and its corresponding influence, over time. Lifelong formation requires relationship and discovery, as opposed to an over-reliance on more and more information and prescriptive answers. This is why many are leaving the church today. Their hunger and stage in development outstrips what the Church is programed to offer, and the maturity level they see around them.

Could this also be a reason why, at this critical moment in history, when authentic believers who have a depth of faith are so needed, they are strangely absent? Though today's Christian has likely attended hundreds of worship services down through the years, many are still unable to translate what they have learned into a Christ-like life. It has produced a Church largely silent in the midst of crisis, unable to respond to critical societal needs, mired in public opinion polls and political parties, and marginalized by much of the culture.

There has to be something more.

Deciding is a book focused on helping Christ-followers discover what's next. It seeks to introduce what discipleship and lifelong development looks like after calling. The Deciding Transition challenges a Christ-follower to go deeper in their walks with Christ by: (1) signaling the shift to issues of *contribution* (major role and effective methodologies), and (2) by exploring issues of the deeper life. The Deciding Transition seeks to bridge the gap between following Christ (calling) and finding one's unique part for Christ (contribution).

Making the shift way from a programmatic approach to a lifelong developmental approach is not easy, nor is it all of what is needed in the Church today. But we believe it is an important step towards being able to see a different kind of believer and a different kind of Church.

There is something more, and there is a way forward.

BEYOND CALLING

Calling is a known topic on the Christian landscape today. It is being used with greater frequency as the Church makes a radical shift toward mission. *Calling* and the missional life go hand-in-hand. The topic of *calling* has become an umbrella term used to encompass issues of mission, vision, vocation, purpose, values, etc. *Calling* was once an exclusive term denoting "full-time" vocational Christian work. Now, calling has application to all believers. Whether in the marketplace, on the campus, in the neighborhood or serving in vocational ministry, *calling* more broadly expresses a life that is focused on intentionally living out the purposes of God. It is said of David, in Acts 13:36, that "he lived out God's purposes in his generation, then he died." *Calling* speaks to a life of intent and focus.

Os Guinnnes, in his book *The Call*, reminds us that: "We start out searching, but we end up being discovered. We think we are looking for something; we realize that we are found by Someone." Guinness also reminds us of words penned in the journal of Søren Kierkegaard,

"The thing is to understand myself, to see what God really has for me to do; the thing is to find that which is true for me, to find that for which I can live and die."[11]

Discerning one's calling is a critical part of the discipleship journey. It can be viewed as a first step in the lifelong journey of discipleship and personal development. As Christ-followers live into their calling, God uses people, events and circumstances to shape one's influence and build in essentials of spiritual growth. The potter has begun the process of shaping the clay (Jeremiah 18).

The further one goes, and the more familiar the Christian life becomes, a growing hunger begins to surface. Longings for a deeper life with God begin to rest just below the surface. These are the first signs of the next stage in the development of a Christ-follower. There is something more, and that something more is called "contribution."

In their book, *Sacred Romance*, John Eldridge and Brent Curtis touch on the passions that often surround contribution.

> *Some years into the spiritual journey, after the waves of anticipation that mark the beginning of any pilgrimage has begun to ebb into life's middle years of service and busyness, a voice speaks to us in the midst of all we are doing. There is something missing in all of this, it suggests. There is something more.*[12]

The research of Dr. J. Robert Clinton (*The Making of a Leader*) revealed that there are a series of six development phases that Christ-followers and Christian leaders alike journey through. Each phase builds off the insights of the former. When seen over a lifetime, this developmental paradigm can be summed up in three, major stages in the running of the race; calling, contribution and convergence (Hebrews 12:1; 2 Timothy 4:7). The Deciding Transition bridges the gap between *calling* and *contribution*.

Where *calling* focuses on entering the race and the initial stages of faith, *contribution* is focused on the running of the race, and going to a new place with Christ. *Calling* serves to summarize purpose and values, defining what is important, where *contribution* fleshes out role and methods, and how what is important gets lived out on a day-to-day basis. *Contribution* is about wider influence that is built upon a deeper intimacy with Christ. Even though we all experience moments of pain, brokenness and wounding, Christ redeems all of life for His greater good and purpose (Romans 8:28).

It is important to note that seeking to clarify *contribution* is not an adventure in ambition. John the Baptist's declaration is similar to the heart cry of one seeking to clarify their contribution: "He must increase, I must decrease (John 3:30-35). More than seeking to do great exploits for God, contribution is about discovering the good deads that each of us have been shaped to do for God (Ephesians 2:10). It is a call to steward one's life and experiences.

Contribution brings with it a new set of challenges.

Life grows more and more complex. Along the way resistance to God's shaping work comes from various voices that surround our lives. Many stop short of pursuing God, and the road to contribution becomes the road less traveled, as many begin to drift off course. The "off-road" experiences of *contribution* often move into unknown territory that were not traveled during days of calling. Ravines of doubt, dangerous curves around life's questions, and steep passage ways over mountains of faith all make moving toward contribution difficult. Time seems to evaporate, energies begin to diminish, and demands of work, family, organizations, friends, and even church all seem to overload a life that once felt easy. The Apostle Paul felt "struggles within and fears without." (2 Corinthians 7:5).

That voice that once seemed so strong and clear in the early days of faith has now become muffled and unrecognizable. The "still small voice is often lost in the challenges and obstacles that come from juggling life's demands. Often the journey of those in the Deciding Transition matches the snapshots of these Christ-followers:

- Bob can't remember taking a day off or having some time just to himself, even just to catch his breath. He wants to hope that someday there will be time to sort things out, but that hope is evaporating under the weight of the never ending things-to-do. And if that is how he feels today, forget about any chance that tomorrow will be better.

- Susan has reached the stage in life when she realizes that she is not the "young-one" anymore. Early clarity and her zeal of working with an on-campus ministry and discipling the hungry has evaporated. Now it's the demands of the job. Everything she does seems to take her further away from the few things she feels God may want her to do. Will she ever really know her role in life, or will she just float in the sea of duties and responsibilities?

- Juan feels like he started behind, therefore he grabs at every opportunity in order to catch up. He always wanted to live a different kind of life and to be involved in things that matter, but this approach quickly led to him saying "yes" to everything. Now he is overwhelmed. While he still maintains his passion and heart for God, he now finds he is unable to say "no" to all of what is coming at him. His fear is that if he makes the wrong choices, he will somehow miss out on what God has for him.

The Deciding Transition and issues related to contribution bring with them a new set of questions:

Of all the things I could do, what should I do?

What is it that I must do as opposed to what are the things I can do?

Am I doing what I am supposed to be doing?

Should I be thinking about a change?

How do I begin to say "no" to the good, in order to say "yes" to the best?

How do I even distinguish or decide between good and best?

What are the few things that I could do that would make a real difference?

Will my life count?

The questions become even deeper as the transition persists:

Why is it often so hard to hear God and know what He wants?

Why is it that God seems to have gone silent?

How do I go deeper with God? What does that look like?

Is it enough to love God, or must I always be doing something for Him?

In truth, do I really trust Christ or do I just desire a life that is secure?

Why all the struggles?

When did life get so hard?

Let's pause for a minute.

How are you doing?

Are we close to describing some of what you have been experiencing as of late? Do you hear your own voice in any of these questions?

There is a good possibility that some of these questions might have hit their mark. They are questions of contribution.

God may be using this in-between time, and the questions it stirs in a different way than you might have first imagined.

Before rushing on...

Linger here for a few more minutes.

Let it sink in. You most likely are in a time of transition.

Give yourself the permission to be present.

Wait. Rest. *Let Him speak to you.*

A FINAL THOUGHT

Jesus often walked away from the busy.

There were times when Christ separated himself from the crowds. It is sometimes hard to picture Jesus walking away from the demands for him to act and the challenges that He faced.

But He did.

Jesus often took a path different than the one the disciples and crowd, wanted Him to take. There were times when more could have been done: more people helped, more people healed, more questions answered, but He disappeared in the crowds (Luke 4:30). In His humanity he often chose solitude. It was where He gained His ability to hear and see what the Father was at work doing. His communion with the Father was what gave him the strength to meet the demands of the crowd.

There is an old children's song that was taught and acted out in Sunday school programs across America during the 1960's and 70s. In retrospect, this simple song appears to be prophetic in nature.

Deep and Wide. Deep and Wide.
There's a fountain flowing deep and wide.

Deep and Wide. Deep and Wide.
There's a fountain flowing, deep and wide.

I think I heard some of you singing along as you read those words.
The critical question is: How does the fountain flow?
The answer is: *Deep and Wide.*
You and I will only go as wide as we are willing to go deep. Said another way, the breadth of our ministry is tied to the depth of our intimacy. Through the course of the Deciding Transition, the focus of God's work is on two fronts: depth *(being)* and width *(doing)*.

This chapter sought to: (1) Highlight life beyond *calling*, and (2) illustrate how the Deciding Transition bridges the gap between calling and contribution.

Chapter Two will introduce the choices that often surround the Deciding Transition. Just like Christ made choices in route to living out His unique contribution, so must we.

THINKING IT OVER

You | One-on-One | Coaching | Group

Below is a guide to help you better process what you've just read. It can be used as you review the ideas personally, as a one-on-one discussion tool, as a small group interaction guide, or as a resource for a coaching conversation between you and a personal development coach.

If you are using *Deciding* with a small group, the following provides reflection questions for your first group conversation.

Welcome Everyone

- What are you hoping to gain from our time interacting around this book? Share expectations.

- Read Text: Ephesians 2:8-10—Let's launch our time by reviewing this key passage. Note that each of us has "good deeds" to contribute, authored by our maker before time began.

Open in Prayer

- Reflect on the following: "The more we get what we now call 'ourselves' out the way and let Him take us over, the more truly ourselves we become."

Reflect on the following questions:

- Review the idea of distinguishing between calling and contribution. How have you viewed/understood the idea of calling? How do you view/understand the issue of contribution? What could be some of the "good deeds" God has authored for your life?

- Transitions can be difficult moments to hear His voice. How clear has God's voice been of late?

- Review the questions related to the Deciding Transition. Which of these apply to your current situation?

- Jesus often walked away from the very activities we find ourselves consumed by. What could be distracting you from clarifying your contribution?

- Before God takes us into greater clarity in our influence for Christ, He first invites us to go deeper in our intimacy with Him. What might that look like for you?

WANT MORE?

Here is a link to Leader Breakthru's website that will take you further on topics covered in this chapter:

www.leaderbreakthru.com/calling
www.leaderbreakthru.com/contribution

2

choices

definition: **choice** / *noun*
An act of selecting or making a decision when faced with two
or more possibilities: the choice between good and evil.

definition: **choosing** / *verb with an object*
To select from a number of possibilities; pick by preference:
To prefer or decide (to do something): To want; desire.

—NEW WEBSTER'S DICTIONARY

How do you expect to arrive at the end of your journey if you
take the road to another man's city?[13]

—THOMAS MERTON

"WELL DONE, THOU GOOD AND FAITHFUL SERVANT." —MATTHEW 25

No matter where I (*Terry*) have spoken, Christ-followers around the world have told me that these are the words they long to hear the most from Christ at the end of their lives. They want to know that their lives mattered, and that they have pleased the One who has set them free. These words come from the Parable of the Talents (Matthew 25:14-30), and are descriptive of one who invests what God has entrusted to them to help extend Christ's Kingdom. The central truth of the parable is that of being good stewards of that which Christ has entrusted to us.

When this story is applied to the paradigm of lifelong development, the words "well done" speak of stewarding one's life story, and the experiences. Life's most precious of all commodities are the lessons and insights we gain through our lives. Words of "well done" are reserved for those who choose to steward and invest what God has deposited into our lives along the way. Stewardship involves making strategic choices. As a Christ-follower enters the Deciding Transitions, and begins to move from calling to contribution, there are choices that must be made.

Choices must be made about aligning
with God's creative, shaping work.

Choices must be made about moving
beyond learning, to new behavior.

Choices must be made to deepen trust,
walking by faith to live a life of obedience.

Choices help to surface the unique
contribution of a Christ-follower.

Choices are an important ingredient
in navigating the Deciding Transition.

ENCOUNTER

"So we who are followers of Christ are wayfarers, and though we have found the Way, we have not yet come to our destination."[14]

As their boats launched into familiar waters, they were in search of the life they knew and the familiar. They were fisherman whose lives had been turned upside down. On this night, they craved the known. Taking on the tasks they had done hundreds of times before, in a place that separated them from the crowds and the turmoil they had just endured.

These last months had sent them into uncharted, unknown waters, navigating life storms with more and more unanswered questions. In this moment their desire was to return to the known. As night gave way to the early morning, they steered their boats back to shore. Though their nets were empty their minds remained full. It was hard to believe that so much had transpired in such a relatively short amount of time. Off in the distance a figure stood across the shore, monitoring their movement.

"Friends, haven't you any fish?"

These were fisherman being challenged by an unknown spectator. This was not something they even remotely wanted to encounter, with everything else that swirled around their life right now. Almost in unison, they all replied a resounding, "No!" "Nothing!" *How did he know about our catch?*

"Throw your nets on the other side," came the same voice echoing back from the shore. "You'll find some there!"

On the shoreline, his silhouette in the early sun was clearer as he warmed himself by a fire. This was an unwanted distraction. Almost in defiance, they flung their nets across the boat to the other side. If nothing else, this would untangle their nets, silence their onlooker and bring some sort of vindication for the lack of results they had experienced during the night.

And then it happened.

Their nets were instantly overwhelmed with fish, so many fish that the catch tested the ropes they had used all night. To be exact there were 153 fish, but the point is that this catch was more than any of their nets could hold. At that moment, some of them of them knew. This had happened before. The one who had voiced the challenge was the One who had changed their lives. John told Peter that it was the Lord. Peter did what Peter always did. He immediately responded. Wrapping his garment around himself, Peter dove into the water, dragging the nets with him. In the midst of accusations, denials and rejection it was Jesus, the Resurrected One, standing on the shore, wanting them to draw near.

As they arrived at His shoreline, hot coals signaled that breakfast and more awaited their arrival. Though their catch of fish was abundant, Jesus did not stand in need of their fish. He was summoning them to something greater than the prize of their catch.

This moment was different from those first moments when Jesus had called them to drop their nets, and follow Him. In that moment, his call was to follow, and commit to a different way of life; to become fishers of men (*calling*). The focus and the direction of their lives were forever changed. But this time, there was something more. This was a next step.

After breakfast, Jesus pulled Peter aside.

What ensued has been preached and taught many times. Jesus' question to Peter *("Do you love me?")* has been explained by many a teacher. The Greek words for the "love" of a friend (*phileo*) and a "love" that is unconditional (*agape*) have been defined. We have heard Peter's responses, asked three times, and we remember Christ's call for Peter was to go and to feed the sheep of the Good Shepherd.

"Peter, do you love me?" (John 21:15-22)

Christ's important question, asked three times to Peter, echoed off the corridors of his recent journey with Christ, and down the hallways of each of our lives who have sought to follow Christ.

A question: *Could it be that Jesus' not only challenge Peter to something more in terms of the task of shepherding his sheep? Could it be that Jesus was challenging Peter to the next level of trust?* Peter had trusted Jesus up to this point, but this next step would take that trust to a deeper level, a level Peter had never gone to before with Christ. Would Peter return to what he knew (fishing) like the night before, or would he move into the unknown and the unfamiliar.

For Peter, it was clear that Jesus' questions were a call to move into the unknown:

- *Peter, will you choose what I have for you, and trust me, or will you return back to what you know you can do on your own?*

- *Peter, do you truly believe in the life I have modeled for you, to the point that you are willing to do what I have next for you and your development as my disciple?*

- *Peter, you have accepted your call, but now will you embrace your contribution?*

JESUS WAS NO STRANGER TO CHOICES

*"My Father, if it is possible, may this cup be taken from me.
Yet not as I will, but as you will."* (Matthew 26:39)

Jesus modeled a life of choices. Daily his life was comprised of choices and decisions.

Each Christ-follower will be required to make choices related to living out one's Kingdom contribution; our story playing its part with in His Story. You and I will be called to decide to align with Him and His purposes. Each of must "take up our cross and follow Him." (Luke 9:23).

*"And Jesus gathered up his courage and steeled himself
for the journey to Jerusalem." —Luke 9:51 (NLT)*

The shoreline encounter with Christ, experienced by Peter and the disciples, brought each face-to-face with the moment when their journeys with Christ shifted from calling to contribution. The challenge of the Deciding Transition is about choices and decisions to intentionally align with Christ, and His shaping work. Often, this will mean a journey into the unknown and into that which causes Christ to increase, and us to decrease.

We who follow Christ have left behind our nets and our own designs for this life, and surrendered our lives to Him. As we have accepted His call, our life has been shaped by the experiences and the people He has brought into our lives. But, there will come a time when we to will stand on the shore and face Peter's question.

Do we love Him?

Will we go to a new place with Christ, and deepen our trust in Him, in order to better understand the contribution He shaped our lives to make?

Contribution involves answering the same question Jesus posed to Peter; "Do you love me?"

THINKING IT OVER

You | One-on-One | Coaching | Group

Below is a guide to help you better process what you've just read. It can be used as you review the ideas personally, as a one-to-one discussion tool, as a small group interaction guide, or as a resource for a coaching conversation between you and a personal development coach.

If you are using *Deciding* with a small group, the following provides reflection questions for your <u>second</u> group conversation.

Reflect on the following quote:

"Sometimes we have to do a thing to find out the reason for it. Sometimes our actions are questions, not answers."—John Le Carre

- What do you hear in the question?
- Where do you sense God might be taking you?

Read Matthew 25:14-30

Reflect on the following questions:

- Review some of the many experiences of your life; the people who have poured into your life, and the unique circumstances that have surrounded your life. What do they say to you?
- Reflect on the story told in John 21 and retold on pages 34-36. What stands out to you with regards to the challenge the disciples faced about moving forward?
- Talk together about some of the choices Jesus made during his life. What do his choices show or teach us as we face the need to make similar decisions in the future?
- In the days ahead, what could be some of the specific choices you might need to make as you seek to move into the next chapter of your life with Christ?

WANT MORE?

Here is a link to Leader Breakthru's website that will take you further on topics covered in this chapter:

lbu.leaderbreakthru.com/products/five-choices

3

the climb

"You would not have called to me unless I had been calling you," said the Lion. "Then you are Somebody, Sir?" said Jill. "I am."[15]

—C.S. LEWIS

The deeper our faith, the more doubt we must endure; the deeper our hope, the more prone we are to despair; the deeper our love, the more pain its loss will bring: these are a few of the paradoxes we must hold as human beings.[16]

—PARKER J. PALMER

I *(Terry)* live in the Northern part of California, in the USA.

I was asked to join the students of my daughter's senior high school class for their annual midnight hike to the top of Mt. Lassen, a mountain peak of 10,000 feet near our home. I said yes not because of my expertise in climbing, but because of my love for our daughter, and a desire to join her as she embarked on the journey of her important senior year. I was literally stunned by this trek up the mountainside, and what we encountered.

Her and I joined 40 other high school seniors and adults for the trek up an incredibly narrow passageway to the top of the mountain. Several times we were dangerously close to slipping and sliding down the mountainside. There were times when the darkness of the night caused us to not be able to see our walking partners, right in front of us. We had no special equipment, no training and were given just two main instructions: (1) stay on the path, and (2) stay together.

I asked my daughter several times how she was doing. The truth was that I actually was voicing out-loud my wonderments about what the two of us were doing as we slowly continued our climb: *What in the world were we doing? Would we really make it to the top?* This was no easy climb. But we made it.

The view at the top was as incredible, just like you'd expect. The perspective of the valley below was stunning. It felt like you could see for hundreds of miles ahead. A thin cloud cover that blanketed the valley below showcased a sea of twinkling of lights. Her and I both were thankful we had made the climb, and as I listened to the students relishing the fact that they had not given up, it made the climb to the top worth every sore muscle. I was relieved when we were back down the mountain, safe on the valley floor below, and I wondered how I would make this same trek two more times with my other two teenagers.

One thing was clear after all that effort and all those questions about whether we would make it, there is nothing like getting to the top. Though a hike in the midst of darkness and uncertainty presented some significant challenges and doubts, the getting to the top, and view from above yielded a prize worth the effort. Said another way: Perspective comes to those who choose to make the climb.

As a Christ-follower, perspective is the by-product of seeing one's life from God's big-picture, point of view. We live situationally but God calls us to live sovereignly, with that big-picture in mind. Transitions are like windows of perspective, creating moments in time when we are able to see our lives in relationship to God's larger work. Like the climb to the top of the mountain, the journey of gaining greater perspective during a transition also presents its challenges.

The "climb" that one makes during the Deciding Transition will take a Christ-follower through issues of past development. It will provide a look at one's core passions and unique wiring, as well as a first look at clarifying influence for Christ in the days ahead.

Below are three tips for the climb ahead. Each will be an asset as you seek to see your life from God's point of view.

1. PERMISSION

It is often necessary to give oneself the permission to take a step back from the activity and the demands of life, and grant oneself the freedom to make this climb. Most are too busy to take the time to focus on one's self. Personal development often falls into the "important but not urgent" basket. Seeing one's life from God's sovereign design is essential, but often battles the needs of others or the demands of the organization for attention.

Permission also involves a commitment to personal honesty. Those who make this climb, and allocate the time and the commitment to do so, need to see their lives through an honest point of view, gaining all they can out of the journey. This would mean giving ourselves permission to ask the questions that must be asked, work through the doubts that have been placed on the back shelves, and resurface the dreams that reality has sought to trample. Grant yourself permission to make the climb.

2. PERSEVERANCE

Gaining perspective often requires a dogged commitment to keep climbing, regardless of how dark or discouraging the trek becomes. There is a ruggedness to the climb that requires perseverance. Most of us struggle with prolonged times of uncertainty. It's hard to relinquish control. To keep moving, even when we feel like we are going nowhere, requires commitment and belief that God is still at work, even in the midst of uncertainty.

Transitions often feel like roads that will never end. The rewards of gaining perspective can be great, but the costs are real. The climb represented by the Deciding Transition, and the shift from *calling* to *contribution,* often can feel very disorienting. It is easy to lose hope, and give up on the climb. Your perseverance will be tested. Sometimes all that keeps you going during a transition is the resolve that the Holy Spirit is still at work, leading and guiding you into all truth (John 16:13). Seek to maintain a dogged determination to keep going.

3. PLIABILITY

In his classic book *Pilgrim's Progress,* John Bunyan documents the character Pilgrim as he faced a series of experiences and challenges that are part of the Christian life. Many of Pilgrim's encounters defied logic, and placed him in a state of being out of control and dependent on God alone. Each new challenge caused moments of questions and doubt, sometimes related to the very purposes of God. The underlying storyline is about whether Pilgrim would remain loyal, and keep moving forward, in the midst of adversity and confusion. As he continues, Pilgrim begins to make adjustments to earlier assumptions and preferences about life. It became clear that in order to keep moving, he would need to grow in new ways, and be pliable, allowing God to shape and form him. In the midst of his journey, he cries out this resolve:

> *This hill, though high, I covet to ascend; The difficulty will not me offend. For I perceive the way to life lies here. Come, pluck up, heart; let's neither faint nor fear. Better, though difficult, the right way to go, than wrong, though easy, where the end is woe.*

The quest to finish well, and hear words like, "well done thou good and faithful servant," will require pliability. Making it to the end will require multiple paradigm shifts, and a willingness to examine, and re-examine what is known. The shift from *calling* to *contribution* may produce one of the greatest learning moments of a Christ-followers journey. "The more we let go of our concepts and images which limit God, the bigger God grows and the more we approach His undefinability… but to avoid mystery is to avoid the only God worthy of our worship, honor and praise."[17]

One final insight about the climb makes reference to some of the terrains that are ahead. Each of these terrains represent new growth and perspective. They are unique to the Deciding Transition, yet not unknown to a believer's current journey with Christ. What makes them unique is the way they combine to orchestrate a new approach to life and ministry in the second-half of one's life. These terrains include:

- *Spiritual formation*— The early days of faith must give way to finding God in new way. In the early days, God chases us, but in the days of contribution, we must chase God. Christ-followers must come to terms with who they are, and who they see God to be.

- *Deep processing*—In the early days of faith, issues of past wounding and the dark side of who we are were present themselves, but God now goes after that which could hold us back as He seeks to reveal our unique, Kingdom contribution. Spiritual authority and influence in the second half is tied to issues of spiritual authority.

- *Life prioritization*—In the early days of faith, we often were called upon by God to say "yes" to the assignments and tasks of ministry. The second half of life and ministry is about learning to say "no." A grid for future decision-making needs to be forged to distinguish good things from the best things.

- *Self-awareness*—In the early days of faith, a Christ-follower discovers their identity as a child of the King, and becomes acquainted with the "true-self." The second half of one's journey is often about encountering the "false-self," and facing issues of ambition and dysfunction that seek to sabotage the life God designed.

Many Christ-followers shrink back from this climb. The challenges and the issues surrounding *contribution* can be both intimidating and convicting. Often, those in the mid-game of life begin a subtle, yet apparent drifting away from the goal to go deeper with Christ. Gradual, incremental, sometimes even unconscious steps begin to move a Christ-follower out of alignment with God and His purposes.

Some who come to the Deciding Transition are in the midst of deep frustration and even anger toward God. His slowness to respond and resolve the woundings from life result in a prolonged time of plateau and arrest in one's development. They often begin to take back of the reins of their life. Like those who left Jesus at the defining moments of his ministry, those who seek to continue must choose to stay (John 6:67).

The foundational of Deciding Transition has now been set. In the pages ahead, you will read a narrative that depicts a committed Christ-follwer's real-life journey through the Deciding Transition. With him, we will come face-to-face with the challenges of this second, strategic transition. In the next chapters, together we will watch the Holy Spirit move into a series of coaching conversations and guide us into all truth (John 16:13). Its time to climb.

THINKING IT OVER

You | One-on-One | Coaching | Group

Below is a guide to help you better process what you've just read. It can be used as you review the ideas personally, as a one-on-one discussion tool, as a small group interaction guide, or as a resource for a coaching conversation between you and a personal development coach.

If you are using *Deciding* with a small group, the following provides reflection questions for your <u>third</u> group conversation.

Reflect on the following excerpt from this chapter:

"Making it to the end will require multiple paradigm shifts, and a willingness to examine and re-examine what is known."

Read Psalm 139

Reflect on the following questions:

- Review what has stood out to you in our discussions related to the Deciding Transition. What has God been saying to you about your life in Him, your contribution and the future?

- How might God be using your current circumstances to begin the process of clarifying your contribution?

- Permission? Perseverance? Pliability? Which of these three could be your greatest strength? Which could be your greatest challenge to getting all you can out of this transition?

- Which of the four topics *(spiritual formation, deep processing, life prioritization and self-awareness)* do you sense God might be wanting you to focus on? Why?

WANT MORE?

Here is a link to Leader Breakthru's website that will take you further on topics covered in this chapter:

lbu.leaderbreakthru.com/products/breakthru-insights

PART TWO

navigating

"Do not look for shortcuts to God.
The market is flooded with surefire, easygoing formulas for
successful life that can be practiced in your spare time.
Do not fall for that stuff, even though crowds of people do.
The way of life—to God—is vigorous and requires total attention."

—MATTHEW 7:13-14 (THE MESSAGE)

WHAT'S AHEAD?

The stage is now set. With some of these initial understandings related to God's shaping work, and the foundation of the Deciding Tranision laid, we now walk through the Deciding Transition of one Christ-follower.

In chapters 4-8, Rick Williams allows us to have access to his coaching appointments as he processed his Deciding Transition. God used each step of Rick's transition to move him into greater intimacy with Christ, and to provide a greater understanding of his unique Kingdom contribution.

4

entry

"We do not find our true self by seeking it.
Rather we find it by seeking God.[18]

—DAVID BRENNER

Let us never hesitate to say,
'This is only the beginning.'[19]

—ANDREW MURRAY

A note as we begin: *Though our example for this narrative is that of a pastor of a local church, he could easily be a business owner, machinist, care-giver, missionary, stay-at-home parent, etc. What Rick Williams will experience, and the insights he will glean, have application to any Christ-follower who hungers to live a life that makes a difference.*

THE DECIDING TRANSITION

"Hey man! How goes the battle?"

My opening words with Rick as we connected by phone.

"Not bad!" replied Rick, "Not bad at all!"

I was excited to connect with Rick again.

We have been in relationship for many years. Rick is a passionate Christ-follower who is also a much-loved pastor. He is defined first and foremost by his life and journey with Christ, and then by the role and job he performs.

Rick has a positive outlook, and is typically upbeat about life and its challenges. Rick had some rough early years, like many, so no one is more surprised than he is that now he leads others as a pastor. He is committed to do all he can to live out an authentic Christ-like life. Stardom is not Rick's goal. Faithfulness to Christ is what drives him. He is focused on living and finishing his life well, being <u>more</u> in love with Jesus at the end of his life than he was when he started. He is no saint, but he has experienced Christ's forgiveness which has set him free to truly live life.

"Are things okay at the church?" I asked.

"Yes," he said, "At least I think they are. You know how that goes."

"Lisa (his wife) and I are doing fine! I really can't complain Terry!"

Rick knew my concern for him spread beyond his job as a pastor, so he spent time updating me on life since we had last talked. As I listened, his words sounded good, but I could sense that things under the surface may not be quite right, and it was probably his reason for setting up some coaching.

Coaching is first and foremost about the person, much more than the issue or problem they face. Having coached Rick (and many others like him) down through the years, I have learned to listen between the words. If you give them enough space, people will often open up and begin to share what they need help processing. In coaching, listening is a greater gift and tool than talking.

"That all sounds good," I replied, "But why do I get the sense that something more is going on? I hear good things, but my hunch is that something is not quite right?"

"And that's what makes you the coach," was Rick's comeback. I could hear his relief, even over the phone, as we continued to talk. "I don't know what you may be picking up on, but I am actually struggling a bit. My struggle is not about the church, or home, but it's with me!"

"It's not because I hear anything bad," I responded, "I just know that all of us sometimes need of place and time to process the stuff of life, and that we all hit bumps in the journey! As I listen, it sure sounds like you have been handling a pretty heavy load these past few months, and it would make sense that you might need some time to unwind and process."

Though we have had many coaching conversations down through the years, Rick once again needed to "test the waters" to see if our conversation could truly be a safe place to let down his guard. There are few safe places for pastors. Once he realized that once again, I genuinely wanted to hear from him, he began to open up and candidly share some of the weight he was carrying. His weariness and struggles came right to the surface.

Up to this point in Rick's journey, he had felt like he could maintain a high capacity of activity and still be able to remain in a deep and intimate relationship with Christ. It had proven to be true in the past. But recently, that ability had begun to fade. He was now beginning to drown in all of the tasks and responsibilities he was carrying. A malaise of unsettledness had descended upon him, and (what made matters worst) he began to lose his connection and closeness to Christ. God had gone quiet and it was time for him to get some help.

As I continued to listen, it was evident that Rick was pushing way beyond his boundaries, and that he was consumed by trying to simply stay afloat. For some time he had been sensing that God was probably wanting to do something new, but he was too busy to stop long enough to find out what the "new" might be. He was too weary to discern which of his tasks were making his load unbearable.

The more we talked, the more I recognized the signs of a transition. Rick's isolation and wrestling with the uncertainties, as well as his diminished confidence and sense of paralysis, all pointed to the reality that something more was occurring. God could very well have been using Rick's uncertainty and depletion to make him stop and assess where he was in his development. As I listened it appeared that Rick had entered the second of the three strategic transitions: the Deciding Transition.

I (Terry) have coached many individuals who are at these crossroads, defining moments in their lives and ministry. Transitions are more than just a tough moment or a difficult set of circumstances. Transitions involve a series of situations and multiple circumstances that are beginning to collide together over an extended period of time.

As Rick continued to share I could literally feel the weight of his heart; loaded down with the cares of so many others. He was weary of not being able to resolve the issues he was confronting. Both Rick and I could see that he was experiencing something more than just a rough patch of time or ministry. He was in a transition.

The Entry Phase of a transition is often characterized by emotions of restlessness, confusion, self-doubt, and isolation, similar to what Rick expressed. Even the strongest of people will still have to confront the end of their capacities and skills. The role of the coach is not to declare the problem, but to create an environment of safety where the discovery of their limits is realized.

Coaches who are prone to simply solve problems can sometimes cause the people they are coaching to miss out on what God might be intending to do, robbing them of their ownership of the problem. Now, my desire now with Rick was to offer new insight into our conversation that might help him to discover the reality of being in a transition.

"Rick, before we dive into all the issues that are weighing on you related to your schedule and all the stuff you are carrying, how about we spend some time unpacking all of what's happening inside of you as you work through all of this?"

There was quiet on his end, and I knew we had hit on something important. It was time for me to give Rick a chance to process the depth of his situation.

"Honestly, I know that all that I am going through has more to do with what's inside of me, than fixing my schedule," He began. "I know I will need to talk about how to handle some of the issues related to being too busy, and re-organizing how to approach my day. But what's been concerning me the most is my inability to connect with God. I feel like I keep doing all the right things, all the things I used to do to draw close to Him, and yet all is quiet. It's been months since I have heard Him speak to me. That is pretty strange for me. This is not something I have ever experienced!"

"Keep going," I replied. "It is obvious we are onto something important!"

"I read. I journal. I listen to worship music. I run. All things that were great times for me to be with God before, and nothing."

"I am getting what I need for my sermons, but that is not what I am needing for me. I can handle all the church stuff, but not this. I never expected a time, when God would go quiet." Rick was pretty vulnerable at this moment. It's never easy to say the things you feel so deeply, out loud, especially when you are talking about your relationship with God.

"I get it and it makes sense," I responded. "You are doing a great job of laying all this out. This is not easy. It's a hard place to be, but you might be surprised how many others have walked in this very place you find yourself right now. We don't hear much about this, but sometimes it is part of how God begins the process of taking us to the next place in our development. You are safe Rick as you share these thoughts. I deeply respect you for trusting me."

The entry moments of a transition often include a time of isolation. Isolation processing is a key to transitions, yet issues of shame or fear can surface and be exploited by the enemy. Wounding and struggles of the past also can surface, causing an individual to feel isolated and abandoned by God in the moments when they need Him the most.

"Why don't we try to summarize what we have shared thus far?" I interjected. "Are you okay if I take a crack at it?"

"I am okay with that," Rick said.

"It all feels to me that the real challenge you are facing is your lack of intimacy with God. You have been carrying a heavy load of duties and responsibilities, but your uncertainty does not stem from that as much as it does from your lack of closeness you feel to God. How did I do?"

"Exactly," declared Rick. "I feel like I am experiencing something I have never felt before, and I am unable, on my own, to find my way to new clarity."

As Rick heard himself summarize his situation, he began to put all the pieces together. He was in an in between time of his journey. And though he had not used the actual term, Rick had discovered that he was in a transition.

The books on coaching say that at this point it is important to continue to ask more questions. But my experience has been different. There are moments when the coach needs to take the "coaching hat" off for a few minutes, and help provide some perspective. Rick needed some insights that could help him better process what God might be at work doing.

"Rick, there comes a point when even the most earnest of Christ-followers get stuck," I shared. "Two thoughts come to mind as I listen to you share. Are you open for some quick input that might help us understand what God is at work doing?" I asked.

"Yes," responded Rick "I feel like I could use the help!"

"First, you can only live out of duty and responsibility for so long. If you keep going on those alone, they will take you to depletion and burnout. In fact, you may be at the early stages of burnout, and not even realize it. God is most likely using this moment to cause you to stop and evaluate what you are doing, and why," I stated.

"Second, your summary tells us that you are not only in a transition, but it also sounds like you could be facing the important mid-life transition known as the Deciding Transition. It is often a prolonged time of uncertainty, and can include a time when a Christ-follower begins to sense that God has gone silent. All the characteristics you shared match issues related to the Deciding Transition. God is most likely beginning to signal a shift away from the early years of calling, and moving you toward something called contribution."

I tried to be concise in what I shared and made sure I put the "coaching hat" back on. I asked Rick to process what he was hearing, and ask questions that would help him process my two insights. His next questions told me that those insights had hit close to home.

"So, how often do you hear this from people like me? Could I have avoided all this if I had done things differently, or was it all bound to happen?" Rick asked.

Rick and I knew that at this point, what we had stumbled into had many more questions than answers, at least for now.

"I think the real point in all of this Rick, is that God has your attention and is seeking to call you to something different in the days ahead!" I stated. "And though you did not ask me this question directly, I do believe you will be able to hear God's voice again. But the days ahead will begin to author a new chapter in your intimacy with Him."

After a time of silence, Rick responded.

"Well coach, you pretty much have hit the nail on the head." Rick sighed. "I thought either I was going crazy, or something pretty significant was going on. I also knew that I could not gain clarity on my own. I had to talk all this out before I could make any sense of it. I don't know if I fully get all of what's happening, but so far I think we are describing my concerns and needs pretty accurately."

His final question was an important one, "So what do I do about all of this? Where do I go from here?"

Unless Rick took responsibility for his situation, there is a good chance he would never experience breakthrough. Jesus used questions to help people take responsibility for their condition. Jesus' most powerful question, used in many scenarios, was both simple and yet profound. Jesus asked those who sought his help: *What do you want?*

It was my turn to respond to Rick's questions with a question.

"What is it you would like to see God do in all of this, Rick? What is it that you want?" I asked.

"I have been here long enough, and I know there is no quick fix," responded Rick, "I want to go after all that God has for me in this transition, and make the changes necessary in order to move into the next chapter of my life and development. I also know that I need a coach who can help me hear God's voice and help keep me accountable during the challenges ahead."

"I think I need to do a couple of things," stated Rick, "I think I need to take a step back from all of this today, and do some journaling. I need to begin to write out what I believe God is doing, and what I initially believe is the purpose for this work. I also think I need to get some time with Lisa (his wife). I think I need her help processing all this, and making sure I am on the right track." These became Rick's two action steps from our coaching appointment.

"I think you are right," I said. "I think both of those are good action steps."

"And Rick," I concluded, "I am not going anywhere. I believe in you, and I will help you discover what God is at work doing in these new steps of your life and leadership."

"Thanks, brother! I really needed this," said Rick. You could hear relief in his voice.

"You are welcome" I responded. "And if its okay, I would like to pray for you." I offered.

"Thanks man, that is what I need most right now!"

THE BACK STORY: TWO TRACKS

Core Concepts

1. The Deciding Transition is a call to focus on being and doing.

2. The Deciding Transition can be launched by either success or life-crisis, or both.

3. The Deciding Transition seeks to move a Christ-follower from a focus of calling onto to issues of contribution.

Biblical Snapshot

Early on in his ministry, Jesus demonstrated with his disciples how life was meant to be lived. Note the path and progression found in these verses:

> *He climbed a mountain and invited those He wanted with him. They climbed together. He settled on twelve, and designated them apostles. The plan was that they would be with Him, and He would send them out to proclaim the Word and give them authority to banish demons.* (Mark 3:13-14, The Message)

Jesus' pattern with His first disciples is one that continues with those who follow Him today.

He invited those whom He wanted… *like He has done with us.*

His desire was that they would be with Him… *like His desire is for us.*

He sent them out to minister… *like the mandate he has given to us.*

He shared his authority to do the impossible… *like He seeks to offer to each of us.*

The pattern from the beginning has been formation along two tracks: being and doing (see fig. 2 on the next page). As we "be" with Christ and deepen our intimacy with Him, it shapes the influence we are made to have for Him. The integration of being and doing produces a spiritual authority that results in the powerful proclamation of the Word, and the ability to move into the spiritual world. The mandate for discipleship today, involves both intimacy (being) and influence (doing).

The years of serving Christ, and the challenges of serving within the Church, can often result in the loss of passion and clarity. Choices will need to be made to prioritize going deeper in one's relationship with Christ (*intimacy*) in order to withstand the challenges of ministry in the second half of life. Choices must also be made in regards to focus and how one spends their time, talent and treasure as a Christ-follower seeks to clarify their service to Him (*influence*). The side-stepping of either track results in a life and ministry sourced out of natural abilities as opposed to Christ's power and presence.

How It Starts

The Deciding Transition often launches in unexpected ways.

The unplanned, difficult, and sometimes wounding moments of life and ministry can catalyze a search for something more; a search for new insights related to a Christ-followers contribution. Even high-point, victory moments can serve to launch the Deciding Transition. Elijah's greatest victory threw him into a time of questions and doubts (1 King 18). Whether through great victory or great defeat, God moves in.

Circumstances that may also accompany the launch of the Deciding Transition include times of:

1. Abandonment: Isolation and aloneness can descend upon a Christ-follower as a result of relational conflict and wounding, or a quiet God who is both distant and not present.

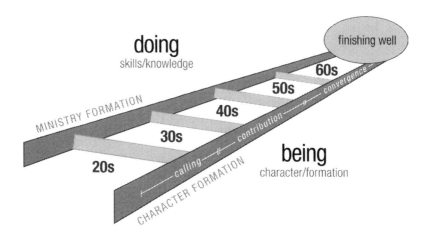

figure 2—Two-track Formation

2. Depletion: Physical exhaustion often accompanies prolonged periods of more and more demands, and the corresponding loss of a big-picture perspective on life.

3. Fairness: Negative events and/or circumstances that happen to good people through no fault of their own, yield deep doubts about God, and resentment over undeserved wounding.

The initial stages of the Deciding Transition typically offer more questions than answers. Natural abilities have run their course. Working harder and smarter can even yield more uncertainty and questions. Answers of the past don't solve the problems of today, and a loss of answers builds a growing frustration. Something has to give.

Jesus did not compartmentalize his life, nor the issues he faced. His ongoing communion with the Father (in His humanity) was linked to His influence and ministry. What He took on, and how He responded, was a direct result of His daily alignment with what the Father was doing. His whole life was lived in an integrated way, bringing together the two tracks of formation; who He was (being) informed how He lived (doing).

Jesus' approach to these moments is noted in John, chapter five:

Very truly I tell you, the Son can do nothing by himself; he can do only what he sees his Father doing, because whatever the Father does the Son also does. For the Father loves the Son and shows him all he does. Yes, and he will show him even greater works than these, so that you will be amazed. (John 5:19-20)

Hudson Taylor, a British protestant Christian missionary to China and founder of the China Inland Mission faced an important transition moment that yielded a focused decision that served to integrate the two-tracks of formation. He declared:

I am no longer anxious about anything as I realize that He (Christ his Lord) is able to carry out His will, and His will is mine. It makes no matter where He places me, or how. That is for Him to consider rather than me; for in the easiest positions He will give me His grace, and in the most difficult His grace is sufficient.[20]

Rick was at the end of the strength and passion he once knew, confronting new challenges to his abilities, and surfacing issues of self-doubt and struggle. Answers would be found from both sides of the track:

- Would he once again choose the many demands and responsibilities of serving Christ over being intimately close with Christ?

- Would he choose to be himself, and give priority to his personal growth and development or would he give in to the needs and the expectations of others?

- Would his Kingdom contribution be the by-product of a spiritual authority that's gained through the integration of being and doing, or would it result from his own abilities and skills?

The Deciding Transition takes Christ-followers to new places of trust and dependency on God. It signals the integration of being and doing.

The entry point into the Deciding Transition is a demarcation point, signaling that the *calling* of a Christ-follower will soon give birth to clarity for one's unique influence and *contribution*.

WHAT'S AHEAD?

Rick reflects on the beginning of his Deciding Transition in his journal entry that follows.

In chapter 5, the coaching begins to help Rick evaluate his current development in light of his transition. The entry phase gives way to a time of evaluation and alignment.

In the Back Story of chapter 5 we discuss how the burden of never-ending activity leads to a quieting of God's voice, and the potential of burnout.

RICK'S JOURNAL ENTRY

Entering into the Deciding Transition for me was like riding on a roller coaster. Ministry had become quite a ride: filled with many thrills, many ups and downs and the need for more speed. As lead pastor of a growing church I experienced some thrilling experiences. Lives were being changed as many people came to Christ and were growing in Christ. God blessed us with new buildings, new programs and new staff members that allowed us to build bridges to our community.

However, I began to experience not only the highs of ministry, but also the lows. The many demands and responsibilities of leading began to have serious consequences. I became very driven by all of the tasks on my daily to-do list. I began to live in a perpetual state of hurry. Living for the applause of many became my default and ongoing motivation. I was saying yes to everyone and everything, which only accelerated an already maddening pace.

This maddening pace was one I knew I couldn't continue. It was having an adverse effect on my relationships. My wife and children were gracious to me regarding the amount of time I was spending in the name of ministry for God, but I knew that something was wrong as I continued to live a driven life. My mentors and partners in ministry also realized I was burning the proverbial candle at both ends. I found myself at odds with those who loved me and truly cared for me. Relational conflict with those around me became a common occurrence and physical exhaustion began to set in.

The biggest struggle for me was the nagging awareness that my intimacy with Christ had waned. The joy and peace that I had experienced in Christ was no longer there. Instead, I found myself alone and distant not only from people but from Christ. A restlessness began to settle in like a low-grade fever; the life-giving relationship with Christ that I preached and encouraged had become a theory rather than a reality in my own journey. The Word of God had become merely a tool to help others instead of bread for my own soul.

I found myself wanting to get off the roller coaster. I realized something wasn't right. I realized I was riding on one rail instead of two: the rail of doing. I knew that I couldn't continue to ride only on the rail of doing without crashing. It was the pace of ministry and the inevitable depletion of adrenaline that left me leading on empty.

THINKING IT OVER

You | One-on-One | Coaching | Group

Below is a guide to help you better process what you've just read. It can be used as you review the ideas personally, as a one-on-one discussion tool, as a small group interaction guide, or as a resource for a coaching conversation between you and a personal development coach.

If you are using *Deciding* with a small group, the following provides reflection questions for your <u>fourth</u> group conversation.

Reflect on the following quote:

"Let us never hesitate to say, 'This is only the beginning.'"
—Andrew Murray

Read Mark 3:13-15

Reflect on the following questions:

- Reflect on the opening of Rick's narrative. Where did you find yourself in his story? What emotions and/or thoughts did you relate to the most?

- Are you in a transition? How do you know? What did the entry look like for you?

- The early disciples' journey with Christ was first a call to be with Him, and then a call to live their lives for Him. Which has been your primary focus recently?

- What could be your greatest challenge as you surrender to Jesus in this season and allow him to reveal your unique contribution?

WANT MORE?

Here is a link to Leader Breakthru's website that will take you further on topics covered in this chapter:

lbu.leaderbreakthru.com/products/integration-being-doing

5

evaluation

You can go along from day to day not noticing very much.
Not seeing or hearing very much, and then all of sudden, when you
least expect it, something speaks to you with such power that it catches
you off guard, and makes you listen whether you want to or not.
Something speaks to you out of your own life with such directness that
it is as if it calls you by name and forces you to look where you have
not had the heart to look before, to hear something that maybe for years
you have not had the wit or courage to hear.[21]

—FREDERICK BUECHNER

A few weeks after our first coaching appointment I got an email from Rick. He had spent some time with his wife, Lisa, reviewing our first coaching conversation and she had given Rick positive feedback and thought we were on the right track. He was ready to talk further.

Rick had a lot of questions about what all of this meant, about transitions, and about where all of this might be headed. But there was little doubt in his mind that he was in a transition. Rick and I were able to arrange a face-to-face coaching appointment when I was in his neck of the woods.

Rick and I met up at a new restaurant near his house and we grabbed an out-of-the-way table on the back patio for a good meal together. We had good catch up time talking about our past, our families and making predictions about Big Ten and Pac-12 football.

I use the *IDEA Coaching Pathway* to guide coaching conversations. The "I" in IDEA stands for "identify." It is important that coaches first identify with the persona and hear about their world before they attempt to identify the core issue at hand. It is important to coach the person, not just them problem. Laying the foundation for a relational conversation often leads to the second part of the "I" step, which is to identify the person's core desire for the coaching appointment.

Rick bridged the conversation with questions focused on understanding how God works during a time of transition, and what he could expect from our coaching conversations. With many of his initial questions addressed, I asked Rick what he felt would be the most important thing to focus on during our session. In coaching, the one who is being coached is the one who sets the agenda.

"I think that I now have a better understanding of what a transition is," said Rick, "and I see that what I have been experiencing lines up pretty well with what you have called the Deciding Transition. So I'd like to begin to evaluate what God wants to do in my life during this time. I actually went back and reviewed what you said about the Deciding Transition in your book, *Stuck!*"

"See, somebody is reading it!" I said, and we both laughed.

"The hardest reality for me to cope with is the thought of having to process my transition while still balancing all of my responsibilities. I can't just stop everything and only focus on the transition," sighed

Rick. "I would like to do that, but I just don't have the luxury!"

It was not hard to see that the reality of being in a transition had now fully set in, and that Rick's focus now shifted to what needs to be processed and addressed.

"It sounds like just knowing that you're in a transition has been helpful," I began. "I am also wondering about your emotioinal depletion and how you're feeling about not being able to hear from God. It seems to me, that as we process this transition, God is at work reshaping you and your leadership."

"That is a pretty good summation of where we are at," said Rick.

"All I know," Rick continued, "is that when I read that transitions can take from three months to three years to resolve themselves, my immediate thought was 'I'm not going to make it.' Somehow, I am going to need to put more gas in my emotional and spiritual tank if I am going to be able to make it."

Rick paused and let his own words sink in.

"Wow! I don't think I have let myself admit all of this until now. I really did not realize how depleted I am really am!" Rick declared.

In my earlier days as a coach, I would have jumped in and felt the need to console, and even remedy the situation. But the more I have coached, the more I have realized that these personal discovery moments are the real value-adding moments of coaching.

Rick broke the silence.

"Well this is an encouraging way to begin our coaching tonight!" he said, "And to think, I even get to pay for the dinner!" That broke the somber tone with some much needed laughter.

Transitions can often become more difficult before things get better. Coming to terms with what has truly been occurring often brings a let-down of emotions and the realization of just how depleted one has become.

"Rick, I can see you are taxed and exhausted. You could be pushing into issues of burnout."

"Wow! You think I am that bad?" Rick responded.

"Not yet!" I stated. "But what I *think* is not important right now! What's important, is what *you believe about you*, and what you are willing to do related to these issues."

"I want to walk you back through my conversation with my wife and then let's come back and re-visit the burnout issue."

"You got it," I said. "Lead the way."

Rick shared with me a summary of his and his wife Lisa's conversations. She has been deeply concerned about the load Rick has been carrying and about his lack of healthy margins.

"She can see what all of this is doing to me, and it's been hard for her to watch. The pace of my schedule has put a strain on our relationship. She and the kids are very committed to me and understand the demands of ministry, but our home life has not been very good lately. She feels we need to figure all this out soon so we can live better into the future."

"She's a smart lady Rick! You married up!" I said. Rick continued.

"I know! I know! Lisa is a trooper. I do not want her to be one of those spouses who ends up resenting the ministry and the Church becuase of my lack of boundaries."

"So what is God saying to you through your conversation with Lisa?" I asked.

"I am at a crossroads moment as a disciple and a leader."

"I must pay attention to what is occurring, and what God is wanting to do in my life." Rick summarized. "I can no longer stay at this place of exhaustion and depletion. Something must be done!"

"Okay," I jumped in. "Let's start there. Tell me what you think are some of the reasons why you have gotten to this place of exhaustion and depletion."

"My best guess is that it all hearkens back to stuff I have dealt with before. For some reason, I just keep pushing myself, as if I have something to prove. I get on this 'treadmill', and as things speed up, instead of taking a step back, I push harder, trying to make things work."

"Do you recognize it when it is happening, or do you often only see it when it is too late?" I asked.

"Usually I see my drivenness after the fact. Then I spend time re-aligning with God. This is why I have been so concerned related to my times with God. Over and over again I have sought Him, and have been unable to get anything back. In fact, I can't tell you how long it has been since I have heard God speak into my personal situation."

Rick continued, "I feel nervous and even some despair. If I lose His voice, and my ability to stay close to Him, then I have lost what I need to lead and be a Christ-follower myself," Rick concluded.

I sat quietly. This set of circumstances was challenging some of Rick's deep, core foundations about himself and God. And it was being used to call Rick deeper.

"Are you open for a comment?" I asked.

"You bet," said Rick.

"I don't know if I can fully prove this Rick," I continued, "But I have observed that in the first half of our journey, God chases us. He showers us with his love and grace, and seems to speak clearly and is easily understood. But at some point (often in the second half of our life) things between us and Him begin to shift. It is not a question of whether God has gone silent. Rather, it is a question of how bad we want to hear and truly identify God's voice. Do we want to hear badly enough that we are willing to lean in, and truly trust what He has to say? Or, do we simply want him just to fix our situation? In the first half of our journey I believe God chases us. In the second half, I believe that God calls us to chase Him."

I paused.

"What if the silence you have experienced is His way of calling you to a new place from which to hear His voice?"

I just let the words sit there on the table.

"If that is true, how do I go to that new place? And, what do I do between now and when I hear His voice again?"

I continued to eat my dinner. I smiled, allowing the tension to increase, then I muddied the waters just a little more.

"Here's one more thought," I responded, "You could be experiencing something documented throughout church history called the "Dark Night of the Senses" or "Dark Night of the Soul." More contemporary Christ-followers have labeled this time you are experiencing as "The Wall." These times are used by God to dig new wells, and bring water to new places within the soul. The future may not be about answers. It could be more about asking the right questions, and loving God for who He is, rather than gaining answers that end up taking us nowhere.

Now we both took a few minutes to work on finishing our meals.

"That is a lot to take in and process," I continued. "As you wonder about all of this, I still remain concerned about your energy and the fatigue you are feeling. Before we close, talk to me a little more about what is happening inside of you. I am concerned about burnout."

"I would describe myself as being in 'survival mode,' Rick confessed. "It is clear that I can't keep pushing. I have less and less in the tank to draw from. I have tried to make some initial changes to my schedule. I also have been backing off of the new projects. Right now, I am just focusing on maintaining what I presently have going on."

"Temporary changes to your schedule is a good start but now all of the answer. What other action steps do you need to take to address some of the deeper issues?" I asked.

"I think I need to talk to my team and let them know what is going on and that I will need time to begin to take care of me. This will mean fewer responsibilities for me, and more for them as I seek to care for myself and sort out the issues from this transition."

"I think I need to go after some of the other things that are holding me back from accepting who I am, and to be able to better acknowledge Christ's love and acceptance of me."

"Keep going Rick, now you are addressing the deeper issues." I said.

"I also think I need to get some time away. Maybe I can go to the retreat center for some rest and reflection."

We worked a few more minutes making sure these goals were achievable and measurable. We set our next appointment and reviewed his take-away from the session, then we prayed.

It's easier to do and harder to be.

It's easier to create tasks and goals related to fixing things or problems, whether at work, home or church. But the Deciding Transition is often more about being than doing.

 THE BACK STORY: BURNOUT

It's easy to be busy.
It's easy to stay busy.

It's easy to convince oneself that being busy is the same as being productive. It's easy to convince oneself that being busy and completing tasks equals fruitfulness, all the while forsaking what is most important.

At some point, our focus on staying busy catches up with all of us, in one form or another. And when it does, sometimes the soul jumps in and calls for a time out.

Core Concepts

1. The Deciding Transition often re-visits issues of past behavior.

2. The Deciding Transition reveals that the demands of life and ministry can lead to burnout.

3. The Deciding Transition often reveals that a Christ-follower needs to go to a new place in their relational depth with God.

Identity and issues of self-worth often get replaced by issues of job, accomplishments and position in the second half of life. Productivity and capacity are valued by both the culture and the Church. In many ways, believers often parrot the culture. It's a lot easier to do, but is more important to be.

Regardless of how gifted, how skilled, or how capable an individual might be, there will come a crossroads moment when limits and drivenness will be challenged by a task-too big, a position too demanding, or a schedule that is too jammed. The construction of a "false self" seeks to build an identity around a toxic culture that demands more and more activity, regardless of the costs.

The more the activity, the more the soul cries out for time. The problem is simple; there is always more to do. Our response is to work harder, purchase the latest book, or to find a better app. Our bodies begin to show the wear and tear of a life out of control.

> We live within a body that responds to stress and in a world that produces it. The potential of stress is all about us. It's in our friends, family, work, our 24-hour news cycle, and every part of our lives. The greater the mobilization of more, the more the stress to our lives, the greater the potential for overstress and, therefore, for stress damage.[22]

Distress, or over-stress, are the seeds of burnout.

The *Evaluation* stage of the Deciding Transition begins the process of peeling back the veneer that has accumulated around our lives, revealing who we really are as well as how far off the path towards Christ-likeness we may have wandered. Revisiting, processing, reflecting and healing are all part of the *evaluation* that often occurs during a transition. Corrections will only be made when problems are owned. One of the great tests of personal honesty is an accurate appraisal of one's use of time, and how much capacity is healthy.

Burnout is a symptom of a greater need.

It is not surprising to see the topic of burnout appear in the mix of the Deciding Transition. Patterns and behaviors ingrained over time can move Christ-followers further and further away from the Kingdom values that once dominated their decision making.

Similar to the frog in the kettle, whose body temperature continued to adapt to the increasing water temperature and was eventually boiled, the Deciding Transition begins to surface warning signals of stress, distress and burnout. Others see it in them, especially their family, but they do not.

In his book *Adrenaline and Stress, Dr. Archibalt Hart* defines and compares stress with burnout. Hart sees stress as the by-product of over-engagement. Burnout, however, is a defense mechanism that occurs physically, characterized by disengagement and physical shutdown. Here is a summary of Hart's contrast between these two states:[22]

- Stress is when there is prolonged over-engagement and loss of boundaries.

- **Burnout is when emotions become blunted and one begins the process of disengagement.**

- Stress is when the emotions have accelerated and become over-reactive.

- **Burnout is when emotional wounding have brought about emotional trauma.**

- Stress is when there is physical impact and damage.

- **Burnout is when exhaustion and physical depletion affects motivation and drive, leading to shutdown.**

- Stress affects physical energy.

- **Burnout produces a complete lack of physical energy and emotional demoralization.**

Stress moves individuals into the early stages of burnout. Individuals often begin to exhibit a sense of hopelessness and despair that is coming from physical depletion. This cycle begins to hinder an individual's capacities to hear from God, and receive help from others.

We at Leader Breakthru have developed a four-step evaluative tool, called the *Burnout Scale*. It is meant to be used to help coach those who also may be experiencing the potential of burnout. Many who have evaluated themselves on the *Burnout Scale* have acknowledged that they are deeper into a time of burnout than they first realized. Burnout is more than just "one moment in time." It is a series of events that moves an individual deeper into a state of depletion.

THE BURNOUT SCALE *Developed by Leader Breakthru*

Adapted from lectures by Dr. Archibalt Hart, Fuller School of Psychology

STAGE ONE:
Physical exhaustion and loss of boundaries. Adrenaline is one's main source of energy.

Typical Response: No acknowledgment—Individual maintains current level of stress and continues to allow for increasing amounts of activity.

STAGE TWO:
Physical exhaustion and loss of boundaries. Adrenaline becomes further depleted. Physical symptoms manifest (fatigue, irritability, lack of sleep, nervous habits, etc.). One's results are diminished.

Typical Response: Denial of situation—Individual makes excuses and justifications while they begin to compromise their standards and values for behavior.

STAGE THREE:
Physical exhaustion and loss of boundaries. Adrenaline is exhausted. Physical symptoms increase (loss of sleep, inability to rest, skin irri-

tations, continued vulnerability to sickness and complete fatigue etc.).

Typical Response: Extreme denial/compromise and lying to self and others—Individual begins to drop their responsibilities, their commitments and even their involvement in close relationships.

STAGE FOUR:
Physical exhaustion and loss of boundaries. Adrenaline is depleted. Physical shut-down begins to occur. Individual separates from activities and relationships (continual sleep, little offered relationally, variety of physical issues and maladies, etc.). Hide and flight become the norm.

Typical Response: Disengagement—complete state of physical depletion, inability to respond to others or offer contribution. Requires extended period of recovery and help from others.

Pause.

Take a moment to reflect.

1. *Where do you see yourself in regards to burnout?*

2. *When did the burnout symptoms begin?*

3. *What are the effects on your behavior of your physical and emotional depletion?*

In Rick's case, the duties and expanding responsibilities had brought him face-to-face with his physical limits. His limitations were contributing to his inability to cope with his circumstances and have a positive view of his future. Rick came to our coaching appointment in *Stage Two* on the *Burnout Scale,* with the potential of heading into *Stage Three* if he had not stopped and accepted his situation. Rick's exhaustion was having an impact on both his physical energy and emotional outlook, and it was what Terry spotted during the coaching appointment. His depleted state was also tied to his spiritual alertness and some of his inability to respond to God.

WHAT'S AHEAD?

Next, Rick moves back and forth between the *Evaluation* and A*lign-ment* stages of his Deciding Transition.

In chapter 6, issues of alignment and refining the deeper work of God become the focus of Rick's Deciding Transition. As God realigns the heart of a believer, He begins to ready that heart for insights about what lies ahead.

RICK'S JOURNAL ENTRY

My journey through the Deciding Transition required a time of evaluation. Questions about identity and intimacy with God were needed. Early on in my ministry I experienced the value of retreats. I would usually begin the year by going away for a couple of days to a retreat center to plan my sermons for the year. It was time for a different type of retreat; the goal would be rest and replenishment.

Fortunately, I was able to share my heart with some mentors and leaders at our church. I shared with them the need to get away because I needed some time with the Lord. They were very gracious and glad that I had a coach who helped me see the need to get away for a time of rest and replenishment.

As I made my way to the retreat center, I felt a little uneasy because my other retreat experiences were about getting something done for the church. This time I knew it needed to be different. I was tired and I was on the verge of burnout. Fatigue and irritability had become a part of my life. Terry had encouraged me to see the need for this kind of retreat. Upon arriving at the retreat center I realized he was right. I was worn out and was in need of rest. I spent the first part of the retreat hiking and resting. I would usually read a lot on retreats; this time was different.

I began to evaluate my identity in Christ. I spent time re-evaluating all of the activity of the previous months and what God was trying to teach me. I was reminded of the truth that God develops us over a lifetime. I had preached that the Christian life is like a marathon; but I was living as if it were a sprint.

During this time of evaluation, I began to slow down and seek God instead of seeking the approval of others. I could feel the heaviness of ministry and activity begin to lift as I began to seek the Lord. Early on in ministry I had bought into the idea: "It's better to burn out than rust out." What I was beginning to realize was that whether you burn out or rust out, either way you're still out. I began to pour out my heart to God praying, "Lord, I want to stay in the race you have called me to run. I want to finish well."

THINKING IT OVER

You | One-on-One | Coaching | Group

Below is a guide to help you better process what you've just read. It can be used as you review the ideas personally, as a one-on-one discussion tool, as a small group interaction guide, or as a resource for a coaching conversation between you and a personal development coach.

If you are using *Deciding* with a small group, the following provides reflection questions for your <u>fifth</u> group conversation.

Reflect on the following excerpt from this chapter:

"Similar to the frog in the kettle, whose body temperature continued to adapt to the increasing water temperature and was eventually boiled, participants in the Deciding Transition can fail to see the warning signs of distress and burnout."

Read Psalm 51

Reflect on the following questions:

- Talk about how surprised Rick was to realize how close he was to burnout. In what way do you relate to his assessment?

- Review Archibald Hart's comparison between stress and burnout. What is the impact of stress right now on your current journey?

- The *Burnout Scale* was developed to re-frame the issue of burnout into a series of stages, as opposed to a moment in time. Talk about the four stages. When have you experienced the stages in the past? Where are you now?

- What do you believe is the connection between the issues of *stress, burnout* and clarifying *contribution*?

WANT MORE?

Here is a link to Leader Breakthru's website that will take you further on topics covered in this chapter:

leaderbreakthru.com/leading-with-spiritual-authority

6

alignment

I am the vine, you are the branches;
he who abides in Me and I in him,
he bears much fruit, for apart from Me
you can do nothing.

—JOHN 15:5

To embrace weakness, liability, and darkness as part
of who I am gives that part less sway over me,
because all it ever wanted was to be acknowledged
as part of my whole self.[23]

—PARKER PALMER

Rick decided to get away in order to be able to disconnect from the daily demands, catch his breath, and explore his relationship with God by trying some new rhythms of replenishment. Rick was now several months into his transition. We connected by phone for this next coaching conversation.

"So, how are you, man?" I asked. "It is good to re-connect, and hear if you are surviving your transition!"

"I am good!" said Rick, "I am away right now on retreat, away from the church and the daily grind. I will be here for a couple weeks."

"Sounds good," I said. "How's it going?"

"Honestly, I am not getting much reading done." Rick responded.

"I've done more sleeping than reading since I arrived. It has surprised me!"

I was not surprised. At the pace Rick had been running I knew that once he stopped it would take awhile to replenish. I have found the same to be true for those whom I have coached in the business sector, missions organizations, churches and stay-at-home parents. Whether young, old, male, female, apart of a team or flying solo, stress is stress, and behavior patterns are hard to break.

The first half of the Deciding Transition can seem slow and unproductive. Most people feel frustrated. They are not receiving the answers or the breakthrough they had been hoping for, and they feel there has been little progress. But, more is going on than they realize. Time spent in the *Evaluation* and *Alignment* stages (see fig. 1, *The Transition Life Cycle,* p. 17) often means facing some of the hard issues that need to be confronted. Most Christ-followers are in a hurry, but God is not. Renewal and replenishment take time. Physical, emotional, social and spiritual work does not follow the clock.

"Think with me for a second, Rick." I interjected. "What would life ahead look like if your focus was not on accomplishing more for God, but living a life of love with God? That's not a rhetorical question. What would actually be different if you accepted God's appraisal of who He has made you to be, and you lived like it?"

"That's an interesting opening question," Rick responded. "I guess my first response is that I am not sure." After a few minutes, he filled in with more.

"I have actually never really entertained not having a focus of doing more. It has always been part of my make-up. I have just approached life based on trying to please God, and to me that always meant doing more for Him." Rick continued. "I don't know what that would mean for me and for my life ahead. My guess is that things might change? Or maybe 'things' would stay the same but I might change?"

"I think that is a good, honest response," I stated back to Rick. "It's hard to imagine how we would respond to a paradigm shift before we actually experience it." I continued. "I know this feels pretty abstract, but, it feels like you are considering what life might look like if you lived life more out of being, than doing. What if we explore this for a few minutes?" I asked.

"I am game," said Rick.

"Brainstorm with me for a moment: What would your day and life look like if you just began allocating more of your time to be with Christ each day, even if it meant not getting things done elsewhere? And I am not talking about starting some new study, or announcing to everyone at the church you are trying something new, but just deciding to begin to take more time, and spend more of your day just with Jesus, just for joy of being with Him?"

For the first time, in a long time, something sparked within Rick. It was as if he was giving himself permission to explore the very longing he had been feeling deep within. This line of thinking kicked our coaching to a whole new level.

Two issues connected for Rick: His deep longing for Christ and his need to say "no" to many of the demands he was facing.

My question to Rick may seem more than obvious to those of us who are not currently in a transition. But sometimes the best questions are the obvious ones. But until you have someone join you in a time of transition, the obvious sometimes doesn't feel so 'obvious.'

Rick reminded me of Matthew 5:17, and the baptism of Christ.

The Father voiced his unconditional love for His Son before the Son had performed any public ministry. The Father announced that he could not love the Son any more than He did on that day.

Rick was beginning to see his situation in new way. His times of *Evaluation* and *Alignment* were surfacing his deep desire to live his life more aligned with God and His love.

"The ongoing challenge in my life has been to believe that God's love for me is not based on achieving results" Rick declared. " I want to start living according to that truth again. I feel that could free me up to go to a new place with Him, and a new understanding of the best way to contribute to others."

As I listened to Rick, it was obvious that something important was occurring. I also knew that it was not being birthed because of something I said or did. The Holy Spirit was taking my friend down a new road of truth. It was a joy to witness.

"You know," Rick continued, "The irony is that I thought I had put this to bed. But it seems that every time I hit moments like these, the issue of self-acceptance returns and my perceived inadequacy and drivenness are the very things that God uses to draw me back to Him. This is incredible!"

"Pause for a moment Rick." I inserted, "This is an important insight. It feels like this could be the reason for the frustration and struggle you have felt. God often goes back and revisits past struggles to help take us to a new place of relationship and intimacy with Him."

"I think what is so strange" Rick continued, "is that I feel like I am back at the same point where I have always been. I have dealt with this issue before. For the duration of my Christian walk I have never felt like I measured up. I was thinking this time it would be something different."

"This is more common than you think, Rick." I stated. "It is especially true when Christ-followers are facing moments of transition."

Rick and I talked about how some struggles we deal with as Christ-followers are healed and resolved quickly, as we bring them to Christ. But there are also core issues that strike to the heart of who we are and that seem to persist and reoccur. Many refer to these issues as part of our "core wounding." They are summarized with descriptions like "fear of failure," "struggles with approval," "drivenness," "insecurity," "struggles with self-confidence" and the like.

The Father of Lies is also the enemy of Kingdom advancement and he does not want us to clarify our contribution. Not only does he sow lies but he desires for us to dwell on past wounding, all of which can perpetuate past struggles and undermine issues of trust between us and our King.

What is actually occurring is that God is seeking to take us deeper in our trust of Him. He is creating a moment where we once again experience His unconditional love and acceptance of who we are.

Brennan Manning notes that our lack of acknowledgment of our struggle to perform is the very reason we see so little fruit in the American Church.

> *If there is a conspicuous absence of power and wisdom in the North American church, it has arisen because we have not come to terms with the tragic flaw in our lives: the brokenness that is proper to the human condition. Without that acknowledgment, there can be little power, for Paul told us that Christ power works best in our weakness. (2 Corinthians 12:9)*[24]

Next in our coaching appointment, I had Rick take out a piece of paper and I drew for him the *Trust Helix* (see fig. 3 on the next page).

The *Trust Helix* is a diagram that illustrates how a re-occurring issue in our walk is used by God to build trust. I explained the *Trust Helix* with a series of statements:

1. As we journey, issues that are difficult to overcome can reoccur.

2. It is easy to feel that we are on the same level of trust and maturity, but note in the diagram how trust deepens every time the issue reoccurs.

3. God uses this issue to take a Christ-follower deeper into dependency.

4. All this leads us toward greater trust and our own lives become more trustworthy

5. During this process, the enemy seeks to implant lies.

6. During this process, the Lord seeks to reveal the depth of His love.

"What is all this saying to you Rick?" I asked.

"Well the first thing I need to say is that I think this is huge. I know we are not done, but for the first time in a long time, I can see some daylight!"

trust

trustworthy

figure 3—The Trust Helix

"I think I am beginning to better understand the meaning behind your words: '*God often needs to do a deeper work in our lives before he can do a greater work through our lives.*'" Rick continued. "I need to align myself again with how God sees me, and experience again the way God loves me."

Because Rick had discovered (re-discovered) this truth for himself, I had little doubt that he would also take responsibility for living out this truth. What Rick needed was a safe place to explore the work God had already begun, and to take the actions necessary to partner with God in this work.

"So, what are your next steps Rick?" I asked.

"It's clear that I need to focus my efforts on deepening my intimacy with God, and allowing him to remind me that his love for me is not conditional on my achievements or success. I also need new insight about how to discern the few things that God wants me to do in the days ahead." Rick continued. "I know I have a lot of work ahead of me, but this clarity brings me hope." Rick realized that he had finally been able to surface the core issue that's been holding him back.

"What are your specific action steps?" I asked.

Rick and I spent our final few minutes working on measurable action steps, which is the final step in the *IDEA Coaching Pathway*: "A" stands for "action."

"How can I pray for you as you work to take these action steps and enjoy your final days of retreat?" I asked.

"Please pray for courage to trust God in new ways," Rick said.

"I am honored to pray for that Rick," I said.

We closed our time on the phone in prayer.

THE BACK STORY: THE WALL

There can come a point in a believer's journey where no matter what is tried, God remains quiet. What worked to deepen one's intimacy in the past seems to have very little effect now. A believer will often feel isolated, abandoned and alone.

And yet, the silence continues.

In Janet Hagberg and Robert Guelich's book *The Critical Journey,* "The Wall" is described as the time when God goes silent. When what has worked in one's journey, up to this point, stops working. "The commitment to time in God's word, prayer, fellowship and time in ministry continues, but there looms a prolonged sense of isolation, and an inability to gain answers to important questions."[25]

Core Concepts

1. The Deciding Transition signals the need for deeper trust.

2. The Deciding Transition seeks to deepen one's view of oneself and of God.

3. The Deciding Transition often brings a Christ-follower face-to-face with "The Wall."

Rick had hit the "The Wall", and he knew it. If you hit "The Wall" during the Deciding Transition, you will also know it. It has the ability to defeat you with its silence. And though you may not know what to call it, you will know that you are at a very different moment in your journey with Christ.

The ancient Christian faith knew about "The Wall." The descriptive titles, "The Dark Night of the Senses," and "The Dark Night of the Soul" were penned by St. John of the Cross and described a Christian's journey when prayer and intimacy are strained. The collapse of perceived meaning and purpose, followed by a prolonged silence from God often left many in the early days of the faith to question God's purposes. The spiritual senses that were used to perceive and relate to God often felt deaden. "The Dark Night" can include some of life's greatest pain; the suffering of prolonged illness, the loss of relationship or the passing of someone close. All of this, and more create a spiritual dilemma that causes a believer to wonder, "where is God?"

"The Wall" most often occurs near or in the second half of a Christ-follower's journey. Many Christ-followers experience a time of frustration and anger as a result of the prolonged silence. Timing could not be worse. Just when answers are needed the most, the voice of the Shepherd cannot be heard. In the first half of the journey, His voice is strong, and his guidance of His followers seems sure. But as the path winds around unknown corners, and into hidden valleys, God begins to orchestrate new ways and practices.

Hagberg offers a developmental paradigm that helps to depict and better understand the purposes of "The Wall." Her *Six Stages of the Faith* she depicts places "The Wall" at a strategic moment in one's discipleship and development. The Six Stages are as follows:

1. *Recognition of God*—A sense of openness and need for the Savior and a greater meaning in life.

2. *Initial Discipleship*—Learning about God; deepening of one's faith and belief system.

3. *The Productive Life*—Living for God; A sense of uniqueness in community and belonging to the Body often coupled with greater responsibility at work, home, church etc.

4. *Journey Inward*—Pursuit of personal integrity in one's relationship to God. Focus moves from "doing" to "being", God is released from the box. The cry to go deeper; the need to develop greater intimacy.

___The Wall___—As one seeks God in new ways, a growing silence and restlessness occurs, often launching deep questioning and faith crisis. Sometimes this produces a loss of certainty and a shaking of one's foundation. A new search for deeper intimacy ensues. From the outside, some evaluate that those at this moment are beginning to either doubt or lose their faith. From within, there is the beginning of deeper, more authentic life.

5. ___Journey Outward___—Life of surrender breaks through into a renewed sense of God's acceptance, love and the deepening of trust. A new season of spiritual authority begins to unfold, accompanied by a renewed concern for others. Life is now characterized by a deep calm and peace as Christ continues to unfold his plans.

6. ___The Life of Love___—Living the life of love for and toward God; wisdom has come and one has gained from life's struggles, compassionate living for others, detachment from things, position and power. Release from a life of stress into a life of holy abandonment to God and what some have called, union life.[26]

Bernard of Clairvaux (1090-1153), a Cistercian monk known in his day as the "Doctor of the Church" wrote many great works related to experiencing the love of God. One of his works was entitled _De Amore Dei (Of the Love of God)_ and it describes the journey toward loving God for God's sake (third degree) as an experience similar to the journey through "The Wall." Clairvaux depicted Four Degrees of love that one must walk through during their journey towards deeper intimacy with God.

First Degree: _The love of self for self-sake._

Second Degree: _The love of God for self-sake._

Third Degree: _The love of God for God's sake._

Fourth Degree: _The love of self for God's sake._[27]

The first degree of love is to love ourselves for our own sake. It is a love that focuses on self-preservation. This love is lived out by protecting ourselves, yet telling ourselves we live under the banner of a loving God.

The second degree of love is where we love God, but for our own sake. These are moments when we know, and are acutely aware of our need for God. We interpret this need for Him as our way of loving Him. As we cry out to God and express our need for Him, we see His presence as vindication of our mutual relationship. "The Wall" is between the second and third degree of love.

The third degree of love is to love God for God's sake. This is when our love for God is no longer based on what He can do, but on who He is. We begin to see God as He truly is rather than just someone who meets our needs. God's character becomes our focus.

The fourth degree of love is reached when a Christ-follower realizes that we are called to live within the fullness of God's love. We each have been created and redeemed because of God's love. When we love ourselves for God's sake, we accept who we are, and live out of who we were made to be. We realize our greatest act of love is to see all of life as worship.

WHAT'S THE POINT?

Most evangelical expressions of the faith, of which I have been a part, find themselves in the second degree of love (loving God for our own sake). Most would likely find it hard to understand love to the third or fourth degree. Our struggle today to move our attention off ourselves and onto others could be more of a "love of God" problem even more than a "love for others" problem.

Clairvaux's second and third degrees of love occur when a Christ-follower moves into a deeper level of intimacy with God. Breaking through "The Wall" is about a call to go to a new place in one's love for God. Effective life and ministry now flow out of *being*. The point of the second half of one's journey is to live a life of meaning and contribution. That can best occur when a believer finds God in new ways.

No matter what Rick tried, his spiritual journey was at a standstill. His ability to push through was trapped underneath his mounds of responsibilities. His hunger for more of God coincided with his hitting of "The Wall," moving him to a new thirst of intimacy with God. In the Deciding Transition, the Shepherd is at work, moving Christ-followers to new pastures. Loving God for God's sake, and loving ourself for God's sake begins to shift our view of God away from who we want Him to be, to who He really is.

TAKE A PAUSE

How long has it been since you have had a deep and honest connection with God?

How long has it been since you have thought about God's love for you, despite all of your shortcomings and struggles?

How long has it been since you have thought about your love for God? Take a few minutes and think about it.

WHAT'S AHEAD?

In chapter 7, we will chronicle how Rick moved from his times of *Evaluation* and *Alignment* (the longest period of time in any transition) into a time of *Direction*, and charting the way forward.

In the *Back Story* we discuss the most powerful word of the second-half of one's life: The word "No!"

RICK'S JOURNAL ENTRY

As I continued through this transition, God brought me to a place of surrender and healing. I began to realize that before I could move forward there were some things I needed to let go of and some wounds that needed to be healed. My natural tendency was to rush through problems with a task-oriented mindset. This time needed to be different. Terry's words of encouragement resonated with me: "Don't rush through this transition, get all you can out of it."

It was life giving to slow down and process what God was doing. I was able to process some of the issues of identity. I had become an approval addict who based my self-worth on the approval of others. If I performed well and heard words of approval, my identity was secure. However, if I didn't perform well I would ratchet up my activity and performance in order to find approval. It became apparent to me that I have always been tempted to assess my identity based on my to-do-lists and my task oriented mindset. I can let busyness become the basis for my self-worth.

God began to help me see the unhealthy cycle I was experiencing. It was rooted in relationships where, as a child, I thought I had to perform and excel to get approval. The wounding was deep and real. As I began to connect the dots, it became obvious that there were some subtle enemies at work in my heart. Terry gave me an exercise to help me identify some of those enemies.

I identified five:

1. *Hurry—living in a perpetual state of hurry*

2. *Drivenness—living out of drivenness instead of calling*

3. *Pride—living for the applause of others; wanting the credit*

4. *Perfectionism—living for results instead of relationships*

5. *Distraction—living for the audience of many, instead of the audience of One.*

As I was able to identify the obstacles that were keeping me from moving forward, God brought me to a new place of surrender and healing, and filled me with the courage to move beyond The Wall. This had followed me through my life and now I was liberated by this life-changing truth: my heavenly Father loves me unconditionally. This revelation paved the way to understanding the importance of learning to say no to a lot of good things so I can say yes to God's best; learning to be me and not somebody else; learning to go deep and then wide.

THINKING IT OVER

You | One-on-One | Coaching | Group

Below is a guide to help you better process what you've just read. It can be used as you review the ideas personally, as a one-on-one discussion tool, as a small group interaction guide, or as a resource for a coaching conversation between you and a personal development coach.

If you are using *Deciding* with a small group, the following provides reflection questions for your <u>sixth</u> group conversation.

Reflect on this summary of Rick's journey:

"My ongoing challenge in my life has been to believe that God's love for me is based on love, and not by me achieving results. And if I again choose to live according to that truth, that could free me up to go to the new place with Him, and the next chapter of understanding my contribution for Christ."

Read Philippians 3:1-14

Reflect on the following questions:

- It often surprises Christ-followers to learn that there are times when periods of silence from God can occur. Has God ever gone silent during your journey?

- Reflect on your relationship with God recently. What are the ways you have used to draw closer to Him? Are there any new ways you have been trying to draw closer to Him?

- Reflect together on the *Trust Helix* diagram on page 86. It illustrates how God revisits issues that you may have thought were resolved. God sometimes re-visits these moments to take a believer to the next level of trust. What is this saying to you?

- What did "The Wall" concept and Bernard's "Four Loves" say to you? Where do you see that you are in your journey with Christ?

WANT MORE?

Here is a link to Leader Breakthru's website that will take you further on topics covered in this chapter:

leaderbreakthru.com/spiritual-disciplines-and-direction

7

direction

The Road goes ever on and on,
down from the door where it began.
Now far ahead the Road has gone,
And I must follow, if I can, pursuing it with eager feet,
until it joins some larger way.[28]

—J.R.R. TOLKIEN

Rick spent many days reflecting and journaling his thoughts before our next coaching conversation. These reflective moments had led to greater times of surrender, and deeper intimacy with God. Rick lamented over how he had let the needs of the crowd drown out his passion for being with Christ. More then ever, Rick now knew that his intimacy with Christ was the true source of his strength.

Rick emailed me and set up our next appointment.

He was ready to process his thoughts, and I was ready to hear about all that had transpired since our last time together.

"Hey Terry! How are you? I've been looking forward to our call today. I have some new insights and ideas to process with you, brother."

I could hear a real difference in Rick. He was upbeat and ready to go after things in a new way. We should never under estimate the power of the Spirit of God to break through and change even the most difficult situations. Coaching the person means allowing the Holy Spirit to take the lead in the coaching process, and focusing not just on the problem, but on how He is using the problem to transform the person.

"I am good," I voiced. "But you sound even better. It's good to hear the new life in your voice."

Rick was eager to share.

"I think I have finally made some real headway. I am feeling better about where I am, and really grateful for the time to process all of this. I can't imagine having tried to go after this without a coach! I really appreciate all of your help in processing my transition. I am grateful, Terry!"

"You are welcome Rick," I said. "It has been my honor."

"I know you are going to ask me what I want to cover today so how about if I cut-to-the-chase, and tell you what I need from our time together, and my core desire for this coaching conversation?"

"I am ready, " I chimed in, "Go for it. Remember you wanted me to ask you for an update of what you have been processing."

"Yep!" Rick stated, "I will include that in all that I will share."

"I have been working my way through our last conversation and my thoughts related to 'The Wall.' I think what we discussed helped me address my issues regarding performance and self-acceptance." Rick reported.

"It hasn't been easy to admit it, but my drivenness was exactly what

I needed to focus on. I am hearing from God again and now I have a sense about how to move forward."

"Great Rick!" I responded. "That has been the big focus of my prayers for you since we talked. My guess is that no one is more relieved, than you!"

"Terry, I so value my time with God. Not having that time is what has made this all so difficult. God has been calling me to a new level of vulnerability and trust in Him. I've been waiting for God to move in and take me deeper, but I think He has been waiting on me. When I realized what was occurring, something new began to ignite inside of me. His desire is for me to chase Him in new ways. To 'hunger and thirst after righteousness.' I can feel myself becoming more alive. My times of prayer and reading the Word have started once again, to warm my heart. I am not completely there, but my intimacy with and dependency on God has definitely improved."

Rick went on to share some of his journal entries with me and how it felt in those moments when God was not close. He was really transparent and let me in on his struggles with fear, insecurities, and concern that God was abandoning him. He kept pushing so hard because he was afraid to stop. He feared what God's reaction would be if he stopped. He feared that others would not need him. He feared he would lose his value to the King and miss out on his part in advancing Christ's Kingdom. It was an incredible time of sharing.

The consistent challenge for those in the second-half of life is one of choosing to look beyond performance, drivenness and success. The second half is often about focusing on the few things that will yield a fruit that remains (John 15:16), and a shift away from the many tasks in order to say "yes" to the few, and most important tasks.

Bob Bufford, in his book *Halftime*, talks about the challenge in the second half of life to move from focusing on many things to focusing on only what is most important: "What's the one thing—not two things, not three, not four, but the one big thing—in the box?"[29]

"What has surprised me is that the choices ahead of me are going to be more about what I need to stop doing, as opposed to the many new things God wants me to do. I think God is calling me to do less and to invest my time in doing the few things that He has shaped me to do!"

"Stop for a second!" I jumped in. "Tell me that one more time, to make sure both you and I heard that, and we begin to recognize the implications of what you are saying!"

"It's true," Rick continued. "Up to this point I struggled with feelings of not measuring up, which meant I must do more. I have trapped myself into thinking that I must prove my worth to myself, and even to Christ, which meant more effort and more results."

Rick continued on.

"Terry, I am not a 'big-name' leader, and people don't line up to hear me speak! But I love to communicate God's Word, and I know that I have gifts and abilities to connect with people, and that they respond to the genuineness of my life. I am beginning to see that my important contribution is to be that person God has made me to be; to be a genuine Christ-follower who seeks to make a difference for Christ in his world, and to be one who encourages and mentors others to do the same. I have finally come to terms with the fact that I need to be okay with being Rick!"

This was the breakthrough moment for Rick. He had known this truth intellectually, but had never fully embraced what this meant for how he lived his life.

"I want to make sure you heard yourself say, 'It is okay for you to be you, just the way you are?'"

I wanted this defining moment to linger in the air.

"Being you… being Rick… is your greatest act of worship!"

I continued. "This is one of the first times I have heard you truly value who Christ has made you to be!" I continued. "I'm usually calling you out on this because you are so prone to under-valuing who you are, your contribution, and the genuine thanks people express to you."

"And I think that is my point!" said Rick. "I think I am finally ready to embrace who God has made me to be, as opposed to trying to be all the things I am not! I think that my future is wrapped up in the choice to be myself."

Rick's voice reflected the relief that had come from finally accepting this truth. "Bottom-line: I need to follow Christ, acknowledge all of what God has done in my life, and see how my story fits into His greater story by being who God has made me to be."

"Way to go, Rick!" I declared. "This is huge!"

Though we shared this conversation on the phone, it was as if I could see the tears of joy that welled up in Rick's eyes. It was time to celebrate a major breakthrough moment. We stopped and thanked Christ together.

"I am convinced," I stated as we launched back in, "that what you have gone through is part of the way God will use you to influence others. Life change brings life change. As you fought your way through this journey to be you, my guess is that it will be part of your contribution to others."

"I know," Rick broke in. "The work we did earlier on to clarify my calling through *Focused Living* (Leader's Breakthru online and retreat process) has set me up to clarify my contribution. I can see how God has been using me to shape others, and now to call them into being who God has made them to be. I feel released and excited to begin thinking about what this means about the road ahead. Since we last talked, I have gone back through the Apex Online Process (leaderbreakthru.com/apex) and have reviewed my first attempts to clarify my unique contribution."

I thought it might help to lay the groundwork for the next step of discussion if I reviewed for Rick some of the core concepts related to contribution. Rick agreed.

Contribution can be thought of as a two-sided coin. One side is Major Role and comprises a 1-2 sentence statement that concisely summarizes a Christ-follower's unique Kingdom influence.

Another way to look at contribution is as a list of *Effective Methods*—a series of 3-5 core functions that are employed as we make our contribution. Major Role defines the "what" of contribution, and Effective Methods define the "how." Both become essential decision-making tools and a grid for the choices that must be made in the second half of one's journey.

Rick reviewed with me his results from the Apex Online Process that he had been reviewing and updating based on the new insights from his transition.

RICK'S CONTRIBUTION

Major Role (The What)

I encourage emerging and advancing leaders to discover God's calling and embrace their unique Kingdom contribution.

Effective Methods (The How)

- *I communicate Biblical truth—with an emphasis on practical application that leads to life-change*

- *I facilitate discovery processes—enabling leaders to get clarity and courage for the next steps in their journey*

- *I coach the ongoing development of leaders—helping them align with God's purposes.*

- *I mentor disciples to go deep then wide—encouraging them to serve and lead from a healthy soul.*

"Rick, you have definitely made progress on all this," I declared. "It feels new, even though I have heard you express some of these thoughts before."

"Yeah, true to form for me, Terry." said Rick. "It takes me a while. But once I am able to spend time and internalize the concepts, I am better able to make them my own, and really move forward."

In the Apex Process, Rick had distilled his spiritual gifts, natural abilities and acquired skills down his Major Role Statement. It took Rick time, and several edited versions to get to what he was now.

"I think the biggest enhancement came in the re-wording of some of my effective methods. In each one I have included an emphasis on someone's personal journey with God. Especially in the fourth method when I state that I want to mentor disciples to go deep then wide."

"So what do you see to be the biggest implication of all of this, Rick?" I wanted to give Him time to start processing the changes that could be ahead, as a result of his new clarity.

"One thing this all means is that I need to start empowering more."

Rick confessed. "I've been so afraid that something would not get done, or not get done right, and that it would reflect badly on me, that I've always jumped in and rescued the very people I have said that I want to develop!"

"I need to stop doing this. It hurts not only me, but it also hurts those I serve. It causes them to not taking responsibility and ownership for the change they are seeking to make. That's why it often feels like it is all on my shoulders!"

"Keep going." I said. "What else?"

"I need to invest more time coaching and developing others. I need to help them discover the solutions, instead of solving all the problems for them!"

"Good again!" I affirmed. "Keep going."

"When someone suggests something new we should do, I need to throw it back to them, and challenge them to consider being the one who responds to this need, if it is really suppose to get done. I need to encourage others to take responsibility so that responsibility doesn't always fall on me. This, in part, is why I became so exhausted."

"I am liking these, Rick. Give me one more, but make it something you know you need to do more of, or start in the future." I added.

Rick responded quickly. "I need to schedule more time away with Christ, cultivating my intimacy with Him. I cannot afford <u>not</u> to do this in the days ahead!" Rick said emphatically.

"Wow!" I stated. "Rick, all four of these are down the right track, and will help you live into your Major Role. Great job."

"I know there are more but I think these four give me a good start." Rick stated.

"They all sound good to me," I agreed! "But before we end this coaching appointment, it would be good to translate these next steps of yours into SMART action steps (specific, measurable, achievable, relevant, time-framed). Your first steps are important steps. We need to make sure you translate your desires into new practices that can be measured over time."

Coaching is about action. It is better to have a few, well defined action steps that actually produce movement forward, than many goals that are ill-conceived and never fully implemented.

"OK," said Rick. "Just for the sake of an example, what if we take this desire you have to coach and develop those on your team, and you take a run at turning it into a more SMART action step!"

"Sounds good to me," Rick stated. "Let me take a shot."

"I am going to set up a monthly coaching appointments with each of our staff to help them process one topic area or problem they want to solve, and coach them to the point of intentional action." Rick paused. "What do you think?"

"Good! But I think we can make it even sharper. Let's bring the 'real world' into the action planning. You know they will also need time with you to talk about their assignments and role. See if you can incorporate some of that in?" I challenged.

"Yep! You are right!" Rick stated. "So let me try again!"

"In the next two weeks, I will sit down with each member of my team, and together we will decide what they need from me by way of help/coaching, and will determine a coaching/development plan, with coaching/meetings planned for the next six months!"

"That's exactly what we want out of an action step. It is specific, clear and measurable. Way to go," I responded.

"Okay," Rick continued. "I think I see what we want. I will work through each of those four areas I stated, and email my action steps to you by tomorrow. I also will do some thinking about what some of the longer-term implications are of this new direction, and be ready to share those the next time we are together!"

"Good work Rick," I declared. "You're getting the hang of all this. You definitely will make a good coach." I said. Rick almost jumped in to deflect my compliment, but thought better of it.

"You are right, said Rick! This is my first chance to really own who I am!" stated Rick. "I appreciate you challenging me, and I am grateful that you did not let me off the hook until we got some key action steps. I need that kind of push."

Together we reflected on the breakthrough, and I prayed for Rick to have the courage now to step into his birthright as a child of the King… and to be himself.

THE BACK STORY: SAYING NO

The *Direction Phase* (see *Transition Life Cycle*, p. 17) begins the process of charting a way forward. One of the by-products of the emerging, new direction is the choices that will be required before the transition comes to an end. All transitions end with a time faith challenge, and a call to new obedience.

Core Concepts

1. The Deciding Transition initiates clarity of one's unique contribution; their major role and effective methods.

2. The Deciding Transition, and the resulting clarified contribution, provide a grid for future decision-making.

3. The Deciding Transition begins to teach a Christ-follower how to say "no" to the good, in order to say "yes" to God's best.

"Major role does not emerge strategically until the mid-40s, after 10-15 years of various kinds of ministry experiences and a variety of tasks and roles. Life challenges and experiences force the need for focus and prioritization."[30]

The more contribution is tested, and refined, the greater help it becomes in future decision-making. Let me illustrate how statements of one's Major Role or Effective Methods could be use to help someone decide what to say "yes" to and what to say "no" to.

Examples: *Decision Making*

The following is an example of a statement of Major Role:

"*To create safe-places, and safe relationships for those who love Christ to discover God's best for their lives.*"

If there was an opportunity or project presented to this Christ-follower to start a new initiative that could help an organization to run more efficiently, this person would likely respond with a "no" based on their Major Role.

Here is another example using Major Role:

"*To communicate the truth of God's Word in such a way that people bridge the gap from knowing about God, to living a life of passion for God."*

If there was an opportunity or project presented to this Christ-follower to teach a class of people who are hungry to grow in their walks with Christ, there is a good chance the answer would be "yes" because of the way it aligns with their Major Role.

In the same way, Effective Methods provide a similar, complimentary decision-making tool. Effective Methods describe ways that one lives out his or her Major Role. Typically, there are 3-4 Effective Methods a Christ-follower employs as they live out their Major Role and contribute to others.

Here is an example of how to use one's Effective Methods to make decisions.

My Effective Methods are: Coaching, Mentoring, Nurturing, Serving

If the job or task presented to this Christ-follower was to help young leaders to clarify their life direction and giftedness, the answer quite possibly would be "yes" because it allows for the practice of their four core methods.

Another example using Effective Methods:

My Effective Methods are: Organizing, Coordinating, Helping, Editing

If the job or task presented to the Christ-follower was an opportunity to serve on the mission team and lead short-term mission projects at the church, the answer, when given a choice would be "no" even though the project itself might be one that the individual values and views as important.

In the early days of a Christ-follower's journey, the common response is often "yes" to the various opportunities that come their way. God uses the early "yes" to offer assignments, tasks and challenges that He uses to shape one's passion and influence. As the journey continues, and a Christ-follower's formation moves into the mid-game, the operative word begins to shift away from "yes" towards "no." This shift is about making decisions, when given the chance, to practice one's contribution. Many of the opportunities at this stage in development are good, and even desired. But, one eventually has to face the issues of time and emotional bandwidth. Finishing well often becomes more about saying "no" than about saying "yes." If a Christ-follower does not learn to say "no" to the good, they will not be able to "yes" to the best.

A friend of mine, Greg Cootsona, has written an excellent book entitled, *Say Yes to No*. In it, Greg helps explain why it is so hard to say no. He states that "our overworked lives and the multiplicity of needs often leads many to embrace more in order to save our careers, our future opportunities and to surface our need for importance. In addition, technology, noise and the glut of entertainment are also primary culprits responsible for pulling us away from the important goals of our lives. It's not so much about a radical restructuring of life, but it is more about carving out times for contemplation, solitude and making choices that allow for times of rest, family life and relaxation. The practice of listening and living out of one's core identity leads to making better choices in life."[31]

The courage to say "no" can also be challenged by one's past journey. Family, home, friends, and early childhood experiences often impact our decision making for the future. Many times, past hurts or wounding set up a series of roadblocks and obstacles to good decision-making and living out one's unique contribution. Here are five factors that often impact decision-making in the second-half of life.

1. *Family background and past pathology*—The environment and issues of health related to your upbringing and home environment in the younger years.

2. *Need for recognition and approval*—The by-product of earlier years mixed together with emotional needs and cultural expectations.

3. *Ambition and the need to validate*—The "ladder-climbing-syndrome" and the need to prove one's worth.

4. *Confidence and self-doubt*—The issue of security and the threat of loss of control.

5. *Organizational dis-health and culture*—The health and dysfunction of the team, ministry and workplace environment.

The Apostle Paul challenged the young Timothy as he struggled with fear and self-doubt. The intimidation of a young leader by older, more experienced leaders is real, and can impact the shaping of a leader. Paul's encouragement was to behave according to his calling, and to not forget the time when spiritual authority had been conferred upon him in the past (1 Tim. 4:12). His challenge to Timothy was to adopt a posture of leadership consisting of love, self-control and a sound mind.; it involved saying "yes" and "no" to that which would advance the Gospel.

Saint Ireneus was a second century bishop who was well known for his opposition to Gnosticism. He is believed to have studied under Polycarp, a disciple of John the Evangelist. One of his greatest statements that served to ignite believers towards passionate contribution was: "The glory of God is a man or woman fully alive."[32] His exhortation was to move beyond issues of ambition, and lack of focus, and to step into a life that reflects the posture of being "fully alive" to God and His purposes. This meant saying "yes" to the challenges and opportunites of touching the world and the church.

In our narrative, Rick was being challenged to live beyond his fears and self-doubt. Pathology need not be the driver of behavior. What others have said or not said to each of us need not be the determiner of our future "yes" or "no."

WHAT'S AHEAD?

Rick now reflects on what has transpired so far during his Deciding Transition, and what it means to wait on God for His answers.

In this past chapter, we reflected on how a transition begins to move a Christ-follower into a time of *Direction* and how one can begin to move forward.

In the next chapter we will discuss the challenges ahead and the faith that will be required of Rick to continue moving forward, through the end of his Deciding Transition.

RICK'S JOURNAL ENTRY

It seemed like an incredibly long time moving through this difficult transition in my life. I had been struggling for months trying to figure out what was going on. The restlessness, confusion, and self-doubt in my life felt like it would never go away. Once I started processing what God was doing in me, slowly but surely God began to reveal the importance of the deeper work in order to broaden His work through me. As clarity began to emerge, confidence and courage started to well up in my heart. God was making clear the way forward for me as I began to realize God's healing work in my life. Now it was a matter of stepping out in faith and following God's direction, and the clarity He brought to my contribution.

Entering into this transition months before, I felt like David when he questioned God in Psalm 13:1-4,"How long, O LORD? Will you forget me forever? How long will you hide your face from me? How long must I wrestle with my thoughts and every day have sorrow in my heart? How long will my enemy triumph over me? Look on me and answer, O LORD my God. Give light to my eyes, or I will sleep in death; my enemy will say, 'I have overcome him,' and my foes will rejoice when I fall."

Like David, God allowed me to go to a place of doubt and questions. Like David, God brought me to a place of surrender, trust and hope. In Psalm 13:5-6 David declares,

"But I trust in your unfailing love; my heart rejoices in your salvation. I will sing to the LORD, for he has been good to me." The breakthrough occurred for me when God brought me to a place of surrender and healing and complete trust in the way He has shaped me to make a unique contribution to His Kingdom. He has shaped me to come alongside leaders and encourage them to discover God's calling and embrace their unique Kingdom contribution. He was helping me to see it was about His Kingdom; it wasn't about building my own little kingdom.

As a result of this clarity about my contribution, I intend now to give the rest of my life being a Barnabas to those around me. This means that I will seek to help develop those around me that God is raising up. This means that I will be sensitive to God leading me to certain leaders that I can mentor and coach. This means that I will continue to give pastoral ministry away in the local church to other leaders so that I can focus in-creasingly more and more on equipping and encouraging leaders in the local church and in the kingdom.

In the end I hope my life will have been spent for God's kingdom as an encourager, coach, mentor, and sage. My lasting legacy will be realized when I fulfill the role of being a Barnabas to those leaders God entrusted to me.

THINKING IT OVER
You | One-on-One | Coaching | Group

Below is a guide to help you better process what you've just read. It can be used as you review the ideas personally, as a one-on-one discussion tool, as a small group interaction guide, or as a resource for a coaching conversation between you and a personal development coach.

If you are using *Deciding* with a small group, the following provides reflection questions for <u>seventh</u> group conversation.

Reflect together on the opening quote from J.R.R. Tolkien:

"The Road goes ever on and on, down from the door where it began. Now far ahead the Road has gone, and I must follow, if I can, pursuing it with eager feet, until it joins some larger way."

Read Joshua 1:1-9

Reflect on the following questions:

- Which of Rick's realizations in this chapter did you most identify with? Why? Where are you in your process of being able to see God's purposes in this transition?

- As you consider issues of Major Role (the what) and Effective Methods (the how), how would you define your contribution and influence to others?

- God shapes us down two tracks (being and doing) simultaneously. Which track has presented the most significant challenge for you?

In what way do they work together to help you understand your future direction?

- What continues to be your greatest challenge in clarifying your contribution?

- In the days ahead, what do you feel you need to say "no" to more? What do you feel you need to say "yes" to more?

WANT MORE?

Here is a link to Leader Breakthru's website that will take you further on topics covered in this chapter:

www.leaderbreakthru.com/deciding

8

the challenge

*Then the LORD answered me and said, 'Record the vision
and inscribe it on tablets, that the one who reads it may run.
For the vision is yet for the appointed time;
it hastens toward the goal and it will not fail.
Though it tarries, wait for it;
for it will certainly come, it will not delay.*

—HABAKKUK 2:2-3

*We are all faced with a series of great opportunities
brilliantly disguised as impossible situations.*[33]

—CHUCK SWINDOLL

Before our final coaching call, I decided to review the notes I had taken during the time I coached Rick through his Deciding transition.

During our first coaching call, we discovered that Rick was well into the Deciding Transition. As his coach, I spent time listening to his situation, helping him (and myself) identify his core desire for our coaching, and I sought to determine what the larger issue was that Rick was facing.

In our second coaching conversation we began to "unpack" his situation and discover the challenges he was up against. I helped in this by asking questions that expanded his understanding of what God was doing.

In our third and fourth coaching interactions we began to evaluate how God might be at work, pinpointing the core issue that was impacting all the other smaller issues. It was here that Rick's breakthrough began to occur.

In our fifth coaching conversation, Rick experienced breakthrough and began to look at the implications of his clarity for the future. He developed a series of action steps which has brought us to our sixth and final coaching conversation. In this final time we will seek to consolidate the gains he has made, and reinforce his new, long-term direction.

The *IDEA Coaching Pathway* (Identify-Discover-Evaluate-Act)[34] served as the guide for each coaching conversation and helped keep our interactions on track. Its simple framework allowed Rick to process the issues that surfaced, and allowed me, the coach, to keep each conversation moving the right direction.

(For more information on IDEA, visit: leaderbreakthru.com/idea)

Though the narrative of Rick's transition may have felt rushed from the viewpoint of the reader, and at times contrived, the substance of the conversations was real, and was similar to what Rick and I experienced. Our coaching conversations took place over an eight month period. Transitions often take longer than the duration of the coaching appointments but the benefit of coaching is often to identify the nature of the transition, and how God works during a transition.

Transitions do come to an end; even if it feels like it never will.

Once the transition is completed, Christ-followers return back to the many demands of life to face a new set of challenges. I encourage those I coach to get all they can out their transition. When the transition time comes to an end, a Christ-follower is left with the insights that come from the work they did during their transition.

"Hey man! How was the family time, and your time away?"

"It was great Terry! It was exactly what I needed." said Rick. "We had an incredible time together! I love being with the family and my grandkids. There is nothing better than getting time together as family. I am sure that it was even better this time because I am feeling more at peace with where I am!"

"Good stuff, friend!" I replied. "I am happy for you on so many fronts. That grandpa stuff is good for the soul. I am sure Lisa is also glad to have Rick back, and for the breakthrough you have been able to experience. We are lucky to each have a family who loves us and who also plays an important role in how God is shaping us," I continued.

"Yes we are, Terry!" he sighed. "I am incredibly grateful for all of what God has done during this time. Transitions are not easy, but remain excited about the breakthrough I was able to see, and where I am headed in the future!"

It was good to see Rick back to his normal self, and facing his future with greater hope and optimism.

Rick's agenda (his core desire) for our final time together was to two-fold. First, he wanted to review the final changes he had made to his Major Role and Effective Methods. Second, he wanted to talk through how to apply his new clarity to the day-to-day challenges he would face as he returns back to the church and its demands.

As Rick began our time with prayer, it was clear that he was a very different man than the one from our first conversation. His voice was passionate once again. His desires were not just focused on surviving, or keeping the organization (church) going, but rather he was focused on living out his life with Christ in all the life domains.

After we reviewed his Major Role and Effective Methods, we transitioned our discussion.

"So, my guess is that you're feeling a little anxious about how all this is going to play out when you get back to church? And you might be wondering if all this will stick as you re-enter the day-to-day challenges?"

"Well, on the one hand, I am excited for what this could mean, and on the other hand I want to go in with a game plan to make sure my time with God, and the other commitments that I have made stay on track! I am committed to not reverting back. I have a lot of experience going back to my old ways and habits. Does all that make sense?"

"Makes perfect sense, Rick!" I responded. "Almost everyone I have coached wonders how the insights they have gained will play out in 'real life.' The truth is that some do revert back to their old behavior and habits. It's hard to know how we will respond to the new challenges and the unknowns until we get there. But the same God who led you through this time of transition is the same God who will lead you into this next season."

"So how do I do all this?" Rick asked. "Do I just have to jump back in, and see how it all goes? Or, do we make a plan and set some goals to help with re-entry? And what about the coaching? Should we keep that going?"

In his questions I could hear Rick's determination, yet apprehensions. "Yes, and no!" I replied. "Yes, you need to get back into the flow of the day-to-day and see how things go. But no, you don't want to face the challenges ahead without a plan. It's important that you have an intentional plan that helps you stay focused, especially in the first 100-days." I continued.

"I wanted to share one more thought," declared Rick. "Plans and setting goals works for me until 'crunch time' hits, and I feel the pressure to deliver. Whatever we do, by way of a plan, I need it to include some way I can recognize when I am drifting off course."

"Here is what I have found Rick," I began. "With a plan in hand, you can adjust. But with no plan, you will most likely return back to your past ways. I have also found that short-term wins help to build long-term momentum and provide motivation to stay on course. If we get some early wins, it causes us to believe we can get more."

There will be moments when past behaviors will re-surface. We go into this new future with eyes open, knowing that the key to moving forward is in our dependence and surrender to the Holy Spirit, and to His ability to lead and guide us into all truth.

"This is not going to be easy!" Rick responded.

"No," I said, "but it is doable!

"The first 100 days are critical, and I recommend that we plan those days out together during our time today."

"So where do we start?" asked Rick, anxiously.

Rick and I spent the next few minutes using a resource called "The 100-Day Plan" offered free from Leader Breakthru (leaderbreakthru. com/free). We first reviewed his desired outcomes, and mapped out his calendar with both goals he needed to go after, and appointments to help him maintain a daily and weekly rhythm for his times with God.

As we talked, Rick began to feel better as he saw his desires being translated into concrete action. There are no short cuts to long-term, new behavior. There are some changes you have to behave your way into, and Rick was facing the need to make intentional choices to live and behave differently.

It was time for Rick to step out, and put weight on all that God has taught him as a result of the Deciding Transition. He now was facing a time of *Faith Challenge.*

"*Faith Challenges* are defining moments when a Christ-follower must decide to put 'weight' on the new direction and life decisions that a transition can produce. God tests dependency and trust by calling Christ-followers to take steps beyond their current levels of growth and faith."[35]

Would Rick allow his past behavior and ways of thinking dictate his actions in the future, or would he courageously begin to live according to his new insights? We just both sat quietly as Rick considered the choices ahead.

"I know what must be done" was Rick's response. "I need to stop re-sponding to all the needs, and trust God to empower my choices, fight my battles, and take care of what I am not called to do. I do believe that He who began this good work inside of me is the one who is at work now empowering my next steps." (Philippians 1:6)

Rick continued. "I used to focus on all the things I should do, but now I want to focus on what I must do. If I do not begin to act in a dif-ferent way, I can only expect the same results. I want something more."

"Good job, Rick." I responded.

"I believe with you that now we have a fighting chance to see something different in the days ahead. You are through the 'eddy' and now you are heading back out into the main stream."

Rick's Deciding Transition had come to a close.

It was also time to bring our coaching to a close. We had completed our agreed upon six coaching calls, and Rick had what he needed to move forward.

"Was our planning and coaching time together helpful?" I asked.

"Absolutely," Rick declared. "Our time today gave me the plan I needed, and a way forward." Rick shared. "And your coaching was key to being able to navigate this transition. I want to thank you, not just for your skills, but also for your friendship over these past months." Rick continued. "I would not have made it without you! Thank you, Terry."

"You are welcome!" I responded.

"Rick, I also want to thank you for the investment and trust you put into the coaching process. Good things happened not just because of our friendship, or my skills as a coach. God did an important new work because you were teachable, and ready to respond to His call."

"There is one final assignment I have for you as we close our time!" I stated.

"Anything for the coach!" Rick chimed in.

"I would like to challenge you to write a one-page closure paper of your Deciding Transition. Write it for yourself though, not for me. It's purpose is to help you summarize the insights and lessons you have gleaned from this latest chapter in your life, and the principles you want to take into the future. I would love a copy of it, but like I said it is not for me, but for you."

"You got it!" Rick stated. "No problem."

"Great!" I said.

"I would like to pray for you as you step into days ahead" I offered.

"You read my mind." said Rick.

 THE BACK STORY: RIGHT QUESTIONS

The second half of one's journey with Christ is different from the first half. It sounds obvious, but it is true nonetheless.

The Deciding Transition launches a Christ-follower into the second-half of life, ministry and influence and to a new place in one's journey with God. Surviving the Deciding Transition is not about coming up with the right answers, but by learning to develop the right set of questions.

In his book *A Resilient Life*, Gordon MacDonald states, "You won't be asking the same questions ten years from now that you are asking today."[36] He goes on to say, "If the way one does spiritual life was formed around twenty-something questions and one is now fifty, spiritual life will likely be obsolete and ineffective."[37]

Core Concepts

1. The Deciding Transition surfaces God's desire that those who love Him would go to a new place in their relationship with Him.

2. The Deciding Transition reveals that there are new questions that need to be addressed, previously unknown to those who walk with Christ.

3. The Deciding Transition seeks to lead the Christ-follower to a greater understanding of his/her identity.

I (Terry) first discovered four powerful questions through training that I received in the area of *Life Planning* with Tom Patterson. In his book, *Living a Life that Counts*, Patterson states that these questions are a significant help for one seeking to better understand their unique wiring and contribution.[38] The challenge to gaining an accurate appraisal of the current state of affairs, and the degree of change that will be required, is the degree to which a person chooses to be honest. Asking oneself the right question, paired with the integrity to answer in a way that is both honest and accurate, can lead to more genuine results.

The following four questions have been adapted to support one's journey towards clarifying contribution and will help a Christ-follower discern what needs to happen in order to chart a new way forward.

Question #1: *What's right?*

What activities or experiences in life are in line with one's contribution, and need to be enhanced, or lived out in greater ways, in the days ahead?

Often times, many positive moments of influence get overshadowed by the pressing problems, needs or issues in one's life and ministry.

Question #2: *What's wrong?*

What activities or experiences in life are sidetracking one's ability to live out of one's contribution, and need to be eliminated or changed?

There are often struggles or difficulties that need to be addressed. Naming what they are, *specifically,* can sometimes begin the process of breaking through.

Question #3: *What's missing?*

What needs to be added to life and work that would cause a person to better express or live into one's contribution?

Often there are things being overlooked or components of one's contribution that can make a significant difference, but they're missing. Adding or addressing what is missing can help address the obstacles. It may just be a few, very strategic things that need to be added.

Question #4: *What's confused?*

What needs to be clarified in order to better live into one's contribution in the days ahead?

What needs to be resolved in order to move forward? Often there are a few critical issues where new information is needed. Sometimes a mentor or coach can offer new eyes to the problem and a new perspective.

If you are in the Deciding Transition, then you will have decisions to make in the days ahead in order to follow Christ and to finish well.

RICK'S JOURNAL ENTRY

Terry encouraged me to write a one-page closure regarding my Deciding Transition. This helped me capture the insights and lessons that God was teaching me, and principles I can fall back on in the future. Here are the insights and lessons I shared with Terry:

Insights:

1. *Live for the Audience of One*
2. *God develops a leader over a lifetime*
3. *Live according to God's definition for my life*
4. *Intimacy with God precedes activity for God*
5. *Lead from a healthy soul*
6. *My self-worth is based on the unconditional love of my heavenly Father*
7. *Ministry isn't my life; Jesus is*

Lessons:

- *I must ruthlessly eliminate hurry from my life.*
- *A leader is a self-defined person with a non-anxious presence.*
- *I will recover my life by getting away to be with Jesus in silence and solitude.*
- *Busyness makes us stop caring about the things that are important to us.*
- *Accept Jesus' invitation to rest when I find myself rushing through life.*

Statement of Intent

In the Days ahead when given a choice, I will:

- *Intentionally and regularly seek times of renewal and replenishment, so as to lead from a healthy soul.*
- *Identify several leaders that I can coach and mentor so they can pass on what has been passed on to me*
- *Continually give away pastoral ministry*
- *Sponsor emerging leaders and extend their influence*

WANT MORE?

Here is a link to Leader Breakthru's website that will take you further on topics covered in this chapter:

lbu.leaderbreakthru.com/products/leadership-dev-101/

PART THREE

interpreting

This life, therefore is not righteousness, but growth in righteousness,
not health but healing, not being but becoming, not rest but exercise.
We are not yet what we shall be, but we are growing toward it;
the process is not finished but ongoing. This is not the end but it is
the road; all does not yet gleam in glory but all is being purified.[39]

MARTIN LUTHER

My starting point is that we're already there.
We cannot attain the presence of God because we're already totally
in the presence of God. What's absent is awareness.[40]

—RICHARD RHOR

WHAT'S AHEAD?

Rick's Deciding Transition is complete.

In the final chapters we will offer interpretive tools that help identify key responses and insights into the transition.

In chapter 9, Rick Williams himself talks about four key postures that helped him process his time of transition.

In chapter 10, Steve Hopkins talks about the "Danger Zone" and the pitfalls that often impact those who face the Deciding Transition.

In chapter 11, Terry Walling talks about issues of differentiation and how the Deciding Transition is used to move a Christ-follower into greater self-awareness.

9

postures

WAYS TO RESPOND TO THE DECIDING TRANSITION

Before I can tell my life what I want to do with it,
I must listen to my life telling me who I am.[41]

—PARKER PALMER

(Rick Williams)

The Deciding Transition was God's call, and challenge, for me to go deeper with Him. This transition caused me to see my journey with Christ in new ways, and afforded me the opportunity to experience God in ways I might not have otherwise learned. These new ways included spiritual disciplines and rhythms I would need to sustain my walk in the days ahead.

In his book, *Celebration of Discipline*, Richard Foster provides a very practical way of thinking about spiritual disciplines, and how they shape us. Foster states:

> *God has given us the disciplines of the spiritual life as a means of receiving His grace. The disciplines allow us to place ourselves before God so that He can transform us. They are God's means of grace.*[42]

Looking back on my Deciding Transition, I see four postures (approaches) that helped position me to be in a place to better experience God's grace and transforming work. These postures have now become a vital part of my ongoing journey, and I offer them as ways to help you make sure that you are able to get all you can out of this important transition.

1. THE POSTURE OF SILENCE

In her book, *Spiritual Disciplines Handbook*, Adele Ahlberg Calhoun describes the spiritual discipline of *silence* as "Freeing myself from the addiction to and distraction of noise so I can be totally present to the Lord."[43]

I typically have found listening to music on my iPhone as a way to relax, and as an enjoyable addition to my runs and workouts. Those times often drew me into God's presence. But, I have also discovered new impact as I entered into those same moments in silence. I no longer used music or the noise of my day to fill the quiet.

Practicing the spiritual discipline of *silence* has become incredibly life giving. It has become my opportunity to intentionally carve out time and space to be with God, and practice rest and quietness. As I do, I am able to break free from everyone and everything, spend time quietly before our God, and become the one who is learning to listen to God more intently. I now notice I am better able to identify the voice of Jesus and I feel liberated from the noisy props I often used to medicate my life.

Silence has also provided a new margin that I needed in order to enter into an intimate time with the Lord. Without this margin it is too easy to be the one who talks. If I keep being the one who is controlling the conversation, then the level of my intimacy stays shallow. I identify with Calhoun when she writes, "Like a can opener, the silence opens up the contents of the heart, allowing us deeper access to God than we experience at other times."[44]

My prayer life had devolved into a monologue where I was typically the only voice I heard, and the only one who talked. As I practiced this new discipline of *silence*, prayer became once again a dialogue with God; a time of communion. The obvious benefit of quieting my voice and my heart has been to be better able to identify God's voice, in contrast to my own. His words are everything to me and my life as He speaks of the love relationship we share, and my position of being "hidden in Him." Over and over He tells me that my being with Him is far more important than all I feel I should be getting done. *Silence* provides space for God to speak.

We live in a world of words.

Henri Nouwen writes,

> *Over the last few decades we have been inundated by a torrent of words. Wherever we go we are surrounded by words: words softly whispered, loudly proclaimed, or angrily screamed; words spoken, recited, or sung; words on records, in books, on walls, or in the sky; words in many sounds, many colors, or many forms; words to be heard, read, seen, or glanced at; words which flicker off and on, move slowly, dance, jump, or wiggle. Words, words, words! They form the floor, the walls, and the ceiling of our existence.*
>
> *It has not always been this way. There was a time not too long ago without radios and televisions, stop signs, yield signs, merge signs, bumper stickers, and the ever-present announcements indicating price increases or special sales. There was a time without the advertisements which now cover whole cities with words.*[45]

You and I have filled up the spaces of our lives with words, to the point of pushing out the realities and truths of God that need more time to be said. More than ever, we need to have God, through our relationship with Jesus Christ, help us create new space and opportunities to really listen, observe, think, and feel.

The need for silence points to the importance of silencing every other voice. It also includes silencing all the voices within that bombard us continually with words, ideas, and ambitions about life so we can hear the voice of the Lord. His is that 'still small voice' that increases in its volume and becomes the dominant voice as I choose to silent my world and my own voice. The Deciding Transition was critical in teaching me to make space for God to speak.

2. THE POSTURE OF SOLITUDE

Calhoun goes on to describe the spiritual discipline of *solitude* as also one of greater importance. Her definition of solitude is the process of: "Leaving people behind to enter into time alone with God."[46] Like the discipline of *silence, solitude* provides a way to relinquish my false self; to disengage from people who look to me to serve particular roles, and from whom I may seek approval.

The words of Jesus in Mark 1:35 provide a familiar picture of Christ modeling the necessity of solitude in his life. "Very early in the morning, while it was still dark, Jesus got up, left the house and went off to a solitary place, where he prayed."

Jesus' example helped remind me of the posture, and the necessity of going to a place to be alone. I have now made a habit of going to a place where no one else is; a place where I am alone just to be with God in prayer. During my Deciding Transition, I made the choice to spend significant time away. This meant time away from family, friends and ministry activities. I too often am consumed by tasks and time spent in constant relationships. This time away was focused simply on spending time alone with God. It was a time to pray, read Scripture and wait on God, but the most impactful side of this discipline was that there was no one else. It is not easy to be alone. Regardless of personality type, being alone with God can feel awkward in the beginning.

One of the discoveries I made was that times of solitude better prepared me to be (and to lead) with others, and discover the few things that God has called me to be and to do. Without solitude, I find that many things are often driving my life. I find that I run myself ragged, and get oh so close to "hitting the wall." Solitude has become a safeguard for me. Times of solitude with God have helped me become more proactive with regard to my schedule and its demands. Times of solitude have caused me to feel that I am living and ministering out of the overflow of a well-nurtured love relationship with God. I need times of solitude.

Engaging people is a wonderful thing, but it also becomes draining and depleting, especially for us introverts. Solitude is like going to a gas station and filling up the tank in my car. It enables me to go the distance instead of running the race on empty. Though I intellectually understood this, I had to experience this truth before I knew it to be true.

Several years ago I went on a retreat to spend time alone with God.

I was struggling with a situation in which someone had deeply hurt me. I made the choice to get away and be alone. As I was hiking and praying along a riverbank, the Lord began to impress upon my heart that I needed to release the bitterness I was feeling. I stopped for a moment and jotted down the person's name and the hurt on a piece of paper. I slowly placed the paper into the rushing waters of the river and watched it disappear. In the quietness of that solitude, alone before God, I felt the burden of that hurt release. I was keenly aware of the power of being alone in His presence, and that this might have never been resolved if I had stayed in the activity of the crowd.

Times of solitude replenish us and realign us with God. Breaking away from our normal patterns and the comfort zone of our routines and relationships creates new space for God to work. It is too easy (at least for me) to make excuses for not getting away for times of solitude. Most often it is not that I can't get away, it's that I don't want to. In the past I didn't place enough value in just being with the Lord. Now I do.

In his book, *Embracing Soul Care*, Steven W. Smith states that,

> *Something happens in solitude that cannot happen in community. Something happens in solitude that does not happen at any other time. In solitude, we experience only ourselves. Community offers us companionship. But solitude extends the invitation only to God, and we share only with Him. In these moments of being 'with God,' we find that he becomes the Immanuel who is truly 'with us.'*[47]

It is in solitude where we find hope and healing. As we abide in Him, he prunes us, shapes us, and speaks to us so that each of us are more fruitful and faithful as we live with Him and for Him (John 15). Times of solitude used to rarely fit my schedule. Now they are life-giving and help me open my life back up to the Lord so that He can renew me and refresh me.

Charles Swindoll has helped define the significance of silence and solitude, "Silence and solitude provide Sabbaths for us, ways of resting with the purpose of drawing near to God. The first is a Sabbath of the mouth; the second, a Sabbath of involvements."[48] One of the adjustments I've made in my life is allowing myself Sabbath times for solitude. I have had to be proactive, instead of reactive, if I was to receive the full measure of this discipline and new posture. Even when pressured by the immediacy of needs, even when *the whole town has gathered at my door,* (Mark 1:33) like Jesus, I need to practice the discipline of solitude and courageously choose to be alone with the Father.

3. THE POSTURE OF RHYTHM

I love Eugene Peterson's paraphrase of Matthew 11:29-30:

> *"Walk with me and work with me—watch how I do it. Learn the unforced rhythms of grace. I won't lay anything heavy or ill fitting on you. Keep company with me and you'll learn to live freely and lightly."* (The Message)

So often we move out of step with the Spirit, doing things that we feel must be done, and living by the ever-increasing pace of activity. Note the call from our Lord is to come and *learn* the unforced rhythms of grace. These rhythms are learned and practiced and they posture each of us to respond to the work God is doing, not the work we are doing.

When it comes to dancing, my wife will tell you that I don't have much rhythm. Every time we go to a wedding reception and get up to slow dance, we start laughing because I can't dance. I end up stepping on her toes without even trying. At my daughter's wedding, I can remember the dreaded father/daughter dance. We started dancing and she started laughing. I knew why; because I was making up some steps she had never danced before. They were forced steps, coming out of my inabilities and desire to please. I've concluded that my problem is not that I don't have rhythm; its actually because I have too much rhythm! *(If you've ever seen the "Seinfeld" episode where Elaine dances, then you know what I mean).*

Sometimes that is the way it is with Christ: using too many steps and trying too hard. The result: we are not staying in step with Him, we are actually blocking the grace He desires to transmit to us each day through the "easy" walk of life together. Peterson talks about the importance of living our lives out of who we are in relationship to who God is; rhythm. We find our rhythm, the rhythm of grace, as we learn to walk with Him, watch him and do life with Him. As we do that we learn the "unforced rhythms of grace." We all need to take this dance class with the Master. And one of the great realities I've learned about finding my rhythm with Christ is that when I am "yoked" with Christ, we move together in the same direction and at the same pace.

The tendency in my life is to try to force the "rhythms of grace" by running ahead of Christ, thinking His real desires are for my accomplishments, and that He is pleased by my greater drivenness and my results-oriented mindset. Or, I tend to lag behind Christ by giving in to the apathy and circumstances around me, believing I can never get things to be right, often stopping dead in my tracks. John Ortberg reminds us that rhythm is something learned, over time. "If we want to follow someone, we can't go faster than the one who is leading."[49]

4. THE POSTURE OF COACHING

The posture of coaching has to do with putting myself into a relationship with one who will walk beside me, and help me recognize God's shaping work. Having a coach walk with me through the Deciding Transition was invaluable. Assuming a posture and discipline of being open to having someone coaching me was critical. It enabled me to focus more on hearing God, and listening to Him through the people, events and circumstances that I was facing. I needed someone to walk alongside me to help draw out what God was doing inside of me.

I have gleaned essential paradigms I knew I would need in the days ahead. I gained new perspective as a result of my transition and the coaching I received. The days following my transition have been lived out differently as a result of the coaching. It helped me to posture myself to finish well. Here are insights related to the value of coaching:

1. *You don't get to clarity alone.* We each need to embrace the truth and importance of "the iron sharpening iron." In Proverbs 27:17 we see this truth, *"As iron sharpens iron, so a friend sharpens a friend."* We need other people in our lives to sharpen us and be a sounding board for what God is doing in us.

2. *We own what we discover.* A Christ-follower needs to recognize the power of discovery. People often resist what they are told, but embrace what they discover. A coach's role is not to tell or teach, but ask, listen and facilitate a process of discovery, helping others "mine the gold" from within.

3. *Listening is about hearing what is said, and what is not said.* A good coach will be listening to words that are said as well as the words between the words. It is important to go beneath the surface of words and help people process what's behind the words.

4. *Asking questions begins the process of change.* As soon as the first question is asked, the change begins. Terry asked good open-ended questions that promoted reflection and self-discovery. I can recall several coaching appointments with Terry where he would listen attentively and then ask a question that the Spirit of God would use to bring me to a place of conviction, clarity, and courage. God has used coaching powerfully in my life.

5. *Both Mentoring and coaching are needed; there is a difference.* Sometimes during coaching, it is important for the coach to share with the coachee what he/she is observing or thinking. Taking the "coaching hat" off and putting the "mentoring hat" on is a concept that Terry introduced me to, and it has greatly impacted my journey. There are strategic moments when a coach needs to speak into the coachee's life.

I was able to better identify the various components of my contribution; my Major Role and Effective Methods, because of my coaching.

Coaching also helped me process how my contribution would play out in the various situations I would face in the future. It enabled me to see a way forward and to embrace God's deeper work in my life.

Finally, coaching also helped me to affirm my identity. As I walked through the Deciding Transition, it was helpful to have a coach listen and ask questions, and to bring me to a place where I was able to grow in understanding my true identity in Christ. Had I not had a coach, clarity regarding my identity might not have come. Thoughtful questions from my coach helped me identify self-acceptance as the core issue of my transition.

These four postures I have just described helped me place myself before God, and experience His grace and transforming work. These postures have now become a vital part of how I am choosing to navigate the journey in the days ahead.

Navigating the Deciding Transition underscored a significant truth that Terry Walling has often shared: "*The width of one's influence for Jesus is in direct proportion to the depth of one's intimacy with Jesus.*"

A FINAL THOUGHT

Mark Buchanan tell us that: "The Chinese join two characters to form a single pictograph for busyness: heart and killing. That is stunningly incisive. The heart is the place where the busy life exacts its steepest toll."[50]

As I came to the reality of the Deciding Transition, I literally felt like both sides of the pictures represented in the Chinese pictograph. My heart is my greatest asset. It desperately was wanting new freedom to express itself. My schedule, and all it demanded, was smothering any hope of that occurring. I was dying on the inside. I crept closer and closer to the edge of burnout. These four postures helped me stay the course, and go to a new place in my walk with God. There were no guarantees as I walked through this difficult moment. But being able to get to that unknown place has meant everything in my life with Christ, taking me to a deeper and more intimate life in Christ. Before the Deciding Transition I recited the command given to each of us to love the Lord our God with all that we are. After having walked through the Deciding Transition, I now practice it.

"'Love the Lord your God with all your heart and with all your soul and with all your mind and with all your strength.' The second is this: 'Love your neighbor as yourself.'" (Mark 12:30-31)

WANT MORE?

Here is a link to Leader Breakthru's website that will take you further on topics covered in this chapter:

lbu.leaderbreakthru.com/products/ten-ways-god-builds-character/

the danger zone

THE CHALLENGES OF NAVIGATING THE DECIDING TRANSITION

The reason why many are still troubled, still seeking, still making little forward progress is because they haven't yet come to the end of themselves. We're still trying to give the orders, and interfering with God's work within us.[51]

—A.W. TOZER

(Steve Hopkins)

Phil was an accountability partner of Terry. He was a leader whose life and influence extended to many people. He was seen as a fresh voice in his denomination, and as an insightful pastor to his church flock. He was an innovator to those who thought the church was irrelevant, and a husband and father to those who needed him most. Phil and Terry met often for times of coffee and challenge. Phil and his wife, along with Terry and his wife, often got together as a foursome for times of support as both faced the challenges of ministry. Little did anyone know, besides Phil, that while all of this was occurring he already had crossed over into the "Danger Zone."

One night when the four of them had planned to meet as couples, Phil's wife entered the Walling home, alone. As she came in it was clear something was desperately wrong. She struggled to share as tears flooded her eyes. She shared a story similar to many we had heard before throughout the Western church, but somehow it sounded new because it involved someone we knew. Phil had just broken the news of a love affair with his female church assistant and announced his desire to end many years of marriage. In that one moment, Phil's words had thrown his life, his wife, his family, the church and the lives of so many others into the depths of confusion, pain and disarray.

Terry coaches pastors and leaders like Phil, who have plateaued and arrested in their development, and often walks them back away from this ledge of failure. But even when it is the focus of your ministry, those around us still slip into the "Danger Zone."

WHAT IS THE "DANGER ZONE?

The "Danger Zone" signals a space and time when a Christian begins the process of drifting away from a life of surrender to Christ. It marks the beginning of an end, a quiet walking away from Christ, from the Church and from accountability to the Body of Christ. It is the by-product of small incremental choices, made behind the scenes, often fueled by issues related to ambition, self-focus and the desire to be in control.

Those who drift into the "Danger Zone" live on the residue of yesterday's spiritual life, and yet continue to function in roles of importance while being void of any intimacy with Christ. A self-focused fog and malaise settles in over their influence and serves to blanket truth and authentic life

Activity replaces intimacy
Performance becomes a substitute for servant-hood
Appearance is of greater importance than the Christ-like life

The research of Dr. J. Robert Clinton (*The Making of a Leader*) reveals that the mid-stage development of a Christ-follower is the most challenging in lifelong development. Many who leave the faith do so near the time when the Deciding Transition occurs. The by-product of resisting God's call for a deeper life are Christ-followers and leaders alike who live life out of natural abilities and acquired skills, as opposed to deeper dependency on Christ. Though an individual may possess title, respect, and influence in the church and the community, a fall has begun. They may continue to receive a paycheck, automatically deposited every week into their accounts, yet few deposits have been made into their life in order to sustain their life.

All believers encounter struggles in their journey with God.

There are times when an authentic relationship with Christ experiences times of question, doubt and discouragement. But, the "Danger Zone" is different. It is a slow drifting away, fueled by lies and self-deception, and comprised of actions that are now justified, where once they were thought to be sin. Many more than we know have hit "Danger Zone" and walked away.

Jesus confronted the religious leaders of His day. He called out those who performed religious activities and wore the religious apparel on the outside, yet demonstrated little or no life on the inside. He declared them to be "whitewashed tombs." (Matthew 23:17) Their decisions became self-serving, steeped in ambition, and had little to do with leading others to a closer relationship with God. They exhibited the same characteristics of those living in the "Danger Zone."

No one is exempt from this drift. The tendencies towards this behavior are in each of us. Choices must be made to avoid the "Danger Zone." What I (Steve) have observed is that there are a series of patterns of behaviors and attitudes that signal one's potential to drift toward the "Danger Zone." Let's review four of them.

The Anxious

This emerging pattern is where stress and needs begin to take their toll, and where the Christ-follower begins to react to the circumstances and the apparent urgency, as opposed to what is truly important. When the urgent and the important are pitted up against each other, the urgent always wins. The next telephone call, text, or email determines their direction for the rest of the day. The desire is to meet everyone's needs and maintain the approval of others. Control permeates decisions. Nothing is left to chance. Approval becomes the medication of choice. Priorities fade. The orientation is *survival*. Individuals are often afraid to stop, which blocks God's deeper work.

The Ambitious

This pattern exhibits itself as a preoccupation with goals. These Christ-followers must prove themselves by taking on more and more. Tasks need to be done quicker, done better, please more people and yield something bigger than before. It all becomes a narcotic. Individuals become focused on objectives, tasks, and accomplishments to the exclusion of people and their needs. It is important that one must always be busy.

The ambitious tend to believe that more books, more information, more data and more resources are the key to breakthrough, rather than more of God. Spending hours on social media, bouncing back and forth from one blog to another, their orientation is *success*. They must succeed because identity is wrapped around results.

The Angry

The angry Christ-follower or leader have often been wounded, abused, denied or held at a distance, leaving them defensive and angry. They are prone to attack those who oppose them, and reject those who seek reconciliation. Aggression, active or passive, is the lens by which every decision can be evaluated. They often need to be in control, believing they must protect themselves from actions of others. If they lead, they believe they are to be *large-and-in-charge*. They work more hours that they should each week, they stress over every detail and they spend more money than they have. Their orientation is *being right.* They seek to escape rather than admitting they may not be right, or in need.

The Automatic

The automatic pattern quickly reverts to going through the motions, doing the minimum of what is required, or what they've always done in order to display their displeasure or lack of agreement. They create a comfort zone that allows them to maintain what is, as opposed to moving into what they need. Behind the automatic pattern is often struggles with personal inadequacy and fear of failure. They stay on the treadmill of activity, but see little productivity. They seek to learn new things but fall back into past behaviors. Their orientation is maintaining the *status quo.* They just "get by" as opposed to trusting God to meet them in new challenges.

These four patterns of behavior open the door to issues of denial, escape, burnout and blame, setting up the migration into the "Danger Zone." Refusal to take ownership of the issues becomes a recipe for drifting away from the will of the Father, and the beginnings of stagnation. Soon, someone else is to blame, or becomes responsible for the problems: the spouse, the children, the deacons, the church, the parents, the past, the leadership team, the community, etc. Blaming others, and refusing to take responsibility for ones own journey with God sets the trap for the "Danger Zone." Justification for behavior soon follows, and behavior contrary to what was once a solid belief system occurs. The sad truth is that this moment often produces words of regret at the end of one's life. The words "If only…" are whispered as they look back.

THE RESULT

The Danger Zone is real.

Those facing the Deciding Transition often see their lives move closer to edge of this zone as they encounter surprising challenges and questions. Resistance to personal change and growth in Christ is not new. Old struggles often become new vices. As these challenges continue they often indicate that something more is occurring than just a difficult moment. Well meaning Christ-followers can slip into patterns much like what we just discussed (i.e., anxious, ambitious, angry and automatic). But the opposite can also be true.

Sometimes leaders and Christ-followers who are strong in character, and have obvious strengths and gifts, also begin to drift. Greg Frizzell writes, "May God save us from our own strengths."[52] Those with great abilities and high capacities often put their confidence in finding answers on their own, and fix things that others cannot. Others begin to see them as "Tim-the-Tool-Man-Taylor" (U.S.A. TV character in the 1990s) and they build an identity of being able to make things happen and work. They acquire the latest gadget, newest book, or adopt the latest concepts as ways to by-pass the problems, all the while they're beginning to drift.

Daniel Henderson warns of leaders who fall prey to this focus. He states, "We have taken leadership, a supernatural gift, and turned it into a finely honed strategy."[53] Skills are often necessary and tools help to build better lives, but the influence that advances Christ's Kingdom comes from the hands of the Master, who shapes character and skills. Psalm 78:72 declares that King David led "… them with a pure heart and guided them with his skillful hands."

THE ALIGNED

There is a different path. Listen to the words and passion of the following Christ-followers:

A.W. Tozer described a longing that begins to surface with prominence in the mid-phase of ministry. *"Thirsty hearts of those whose longings have been wakened by the touch of God within… that there is something more."*[54]

Richard Foster, author of *Celebration of Discipline* writes: *"It is not our intent to simply shape our exteriors. Rather we want to go to the heart of the matter. God works out of who we are. To simply 'do the right things' makes for a shallow, inauthentic ministry. We must wrestle with ourselves, recognizing and embracing God's shaping work."*[55]

Ken Blanchard and Phil Hodges who authored the book, *Lead Like Jesus,* remind us *"God is not looking for leaders but for servants who will let Him be the leader."*[56]

Kyle Idleman writes in his book *Not a Fan,* *"There is no substitute for humbling yourself before God."*[57]

For many years Elizabeth Elliot has been calling us deeper, especially in the crossroad moments of transition.

"Leaders (Christ-followers) are measured by how they sacrifice, not by how much they gain. When the will of God cuts across the will of a person, somebody has to die. Leaders are meant to be losers—losers of ourselves and losers of our rights. The best way to find out whether you really have a servant's heart is to see what your reaction is when somebody treats you like one."[58]

The aligned life is the surrendered life.

God's call to go deeper is a choice to move to a new place of surrender, and begin to discover the work that Christ has been already at work doing. Alignment brings with it an increased spiritual authority, and a lessening of our dependence on natural ability or giftedness.[59] Jesus called us to alignment by saying, *"take up my yoke and learn from me"* and *"abide in me."* (Matthew 11:25–30; John 15) Aligned leaders have come to understand that the Father will not share His glory with another. (1 Corinthians 1:29; Isaiah 42:8) Increasingly they understand John the Baptist's declaration, *"He must increase, but I must decrease;"* (John 3:30). Alignment becomes a way of life.

As followers of Christ choose alignment, they are *"conformed to the image of His Son."* (Romans 8:29) As they are conformed to the original (Jesus), they begin to reproduce essential features of the original (Jesus), and others follow. A deeper, more intimate walk with Christ produces a greater *"fragrance of Christ."* (2 Corinthians 2:14-15) It is not the wealth of information, but the depth of intimacy that changes our lives, and those God entrust to us.

PATTERNS v. PRESENCE

Anxious? Ambitious? Angered? Automatic?

The Deciding Transition presents the challenge to move away from the "Danger Zone" and towards a new place of alignment and dependency on Christ. Patterns of resistance must be challenged in the days ahead. Choices will need to be made that align us more with the will of the Father, and less to the responses of the flesh. Mike Harland of LifeWay Worship, says: "God will never give you a template for life or ministry that will eliminate absolute dependence on Him, or eliminate the need for a daily conversation with Him."[60] (1 Chronicles 14:8-17)

This chapter has sought to heighten our need for a renewed alignment with Christ. This comes to the forefront during the Deciding Transition. Our nature is to seek to replace surrender and alignment with our knowledge, abilities and strategies, making us dangerous and able to sidetrack God's work. But God intervenes. And by His grace, he uses these moments to deepen our dependency on Him.

Jesus modeled the aligned life.

In John 5:19–20, He replied to those questioning Him by saying, *"... The Son is not able to do anything on His own, but only what He sees the Father doing."* (See also John 4:34; 7:16–17; 8:28–29; 14:10) During all those times when the Scriptures mention Jesus praying, He was doing more than checking *"devotions"* off his to-do list. He was aligning Himself with the work of the Father, receiving His ministry. (Matthew 14:23; 26:36–42; Mark 1:35; 6:46–47; Luke 5:16; 6:12; 9:18, 28; Hebrews 5:7)

Paul described the aligned life:

"So here's what I want you to do, God helping you:

Take your everyday, ordinary life—your sleeping, eating, going-to-work, and walking-around life—and place it before God as an offering. Embracing what God does for you is the best thing you can do for Him. Don't become so well adjusted to your culture that you fit into it without even thinking. Instead, fix your attention on God. You'll be changed from the inside out. Readily recognize what he wants from you, and quickly respond to it. Unlike the culture around you, always dragging you down to its level of immaturity, God brings the best out of you, develops well-formed maturity in you." (Romans 12:1-2, *The Message*, underlining added)

Paul David Tripp writes about what it means to live out the aligned life, and experience God's work of grace:

He is rescuing you from thinking that you can live the life you were meant to live while relying on the inadequate resources of your wisdom, experience, righteousness, and strength; and is transforming you into a person who lives a life shaped by radical God-centered faith. He is the ultimate craftsman, and we are His clay. He will not take us off His wheel until His fingers have molded us into those who really do believe and do not doubt.[61]

Our prayers need to be more than cries for help. Ours prayers must be cries of total surrender.

God we surrender. Though we feel so powerless and out of control, we chose to align our live first to you, and then your work.

The Father responds to our surrender with new revelation. We *receive* a fresh glimpse of what the Lord Himself. Peter writes: "Christ Jesus, will *personally* restore, establish, strengthen, and support you." (1 Peter 5:5-10, emphasis added) Jesus becomes our life. We begin to love God not for our sake, but for God's sake. (1 Corinthians 1:30)

And the bonus of the aligned life?

We get a "box seat" to watch the Father at work, as He takes our lives and does far greater than anything we could ever ask or think (Ephesians 3:20).

"Thank you, Father that we get to surrender to what you are already at work doing. And as we witness what only you can do, we again get the chance to marvel at who You are, and Your glory."

WANT MORE?

Here is a link to Leader Breakthru's website that will take you further on topics covered in this chapter:

lbu.leaderbreakthru.com/products/understanding-mentoring/

11

differentiation

*"Without question the single variable of families,
congregations and synagogues that have survived and flourished
from those that disintegrated was the presence
of what I refer to as a well differentiated leader.*[62]

—EDWIN FRIEDMAN

Edwin Friedman, author of the book *The Failure of Nerve*, was a Rabi who lectured on *Family Systems Theory*. Friedman has taken the research of Dr. Murray Bowen and applied and its relevance to congregational and synagogue life. According to Murray Bowen who is considered the father of Family Systems Theory, the more differentiated a person becomes, the more he or she can be "an individual, while in emotional contact with another person or the group. Conversely, the less differentiated we are from destructive influences, both externally and internally, the less able we are to relate closely to another person, our mate or our children."[63]

Friedman's seminal work *Generation to Generation*, was written to help better understand the challenges of leading and working to bring about change in families, churches and synagogues. Friedman holds that to make a difference, it would require that those who seek to influence these environments should be:

- Self-differentiated

- Non-anxious

- Present with those they lead

Friedman defines a leader as a "self-defined person with a non-anxious presence."[64]

He describes the concepts of "differentiation" and becoming "self-differentiated" as the journey of moving into greater self-knowledge and self-awareness. Being 'self-defined' is about being someone who is less likely to become lost in the anxious activities of the many environments that swirl around them. Self-differentiated individuals are better able to manage their reactivity to others, and therefore are able to take a stand at the risk of displeasing others.

In one way or another, differentiation becomes an issue surrounding the Deciding Transition. Clarifying personal contribution must often confront the reactions of others. Each of us will take a walk across the bridge we have just read about. Though there is a stark ending to this fable, there is a reality to the storyline that is true. The Deciding Transition ushers in a new understanding, both of who we are as a Christ-follower, and who we are not.

The following is a fable written by Edwin Friedman that illustrate the truth that surrounds self-differentiation. A fable is a short story, created to help illustrate a deeper truth or moral. Before rushing to conclusions related to the message of this fable, and how it relates to the topic of contribution and the Deciding Transition, give yourself permission and freedom to simply experience the narrative. After you complete the reading, we will reflect together on why it has been included and its relevance to our discussions related to contribution.

THE BRIDGE *by Edwin H. Friedman*

There was a man who had given much thought to what he wanted from life.

He had experienced many moods and trials. He had experimented with different ways of living, and he had his share of both success and failure. At last, he began to see clearly where he wanted to go. Diligently, he searched for the right opportunity.

Sometimes he came close, only to be pushed away.

Often he applied all his strength and imagination, only to find the path hopelessly blocked.

And then at last it came. But the opportunity would not wait. It would be made available only for a short time. If it was seen that he was not committed, the opportunity would not come again. Eager to arrive, he started on his journey.

With each step, he wanted to move faster; with each thought about his goal, his heart beat quicker; with each vision of what lay ahead, he found renewed vigor. Strength that had left him since his early youth returned, and desires, all kinds of desires, reawakened from their long-dormant positions.

Hurrying along, he came upon a bridge built high above a river in order to protect it from the floods of spring. He started across. Then he noticed someone coming from the opposite direction.

As they moved closer, it seemed as though the other was coming to greet him. He could see clearly, however, that he did not know this other who was dressed similarly except for something tied around his waist.

When they were within hailing distance, he could see that what the other had about his waist was a rope. It was wrapped around him many times and probably, if extended, would reach a length of 30 feet. The other began to uncurl the rope, and, just as they were coming close, the stranger said, "Pardon me, would you be so kind as to hold the end for a moment?"

Surprised by this politely phrased but curious request, he agreed without a thought, reached out, and took it.

"Thank you," said the other, who then added, "two hands now, and remember, hold tight." Whereupon, the other jumped off the bridge.

Quickly, the free-falling body hurtled the distance of the rope's length, and from the bridge the man abruptly felt the pull. Instinctively, he held tight and was almost dragged over the side. He managed to brace himself against the edge, however, and after having caught his breath, looked down at the other dangling, close to oblivion.

"What are you trying to do?" he yelled.

Just hold tight," said the other.

"This is ridiculous," the man thought and began trying to haul the other in. He could not get the leverage, however. It was as though the weight of the other person and the length of the rope had been carefully calculated in advance so that together they created a counterweight just beyond his strength to bring the other back to safety.

"Why did you do this?" the man called out.

"Remember," said the other, "if you let go, I will be lost."

"But I cannot pull you up," the man cried.

"I am your responsibility," said the other.

"Well, I did not ask for it," the man said.

"If you let go, I am lost," repeated the other.

He began to look around for help. But there was no one. How long would he have to wait? Why did this happen to befall him now, just as he was on the verge of true purpose?

He examined the side, searching for a place to tie the rope.

Some protrusion perhaps, or maybe a hole in the boards. But the railing was unusually uniform in shape; there were no spaces between the boards. There was no way to get rid of this newfound burden, even temporarily.

"What do you want?" he asked the other hanging below.

"Just your help," the other answered.

"How can I help? I cannot pull you in, and there is no place to tie the rope so that I can go and find someone to help me help you."

"I know that. Just hang on; that will be enough. Tie the rope around your waist; it will be easier." Fearing that his arms could not hold out much longer, he tied the rope around his waist.

"Why did you do this?" he asked again. "Don't you see what you have done? What possible purpose could you have had in mind?"

"Just remember," said the other, "my life is in your hands."

What should he do? "If I let go, all my life I will know that I let this other die. If I stay, I risk losing my momentum toward my own long-sought-after direction. Either way this will haunt me forever." With ironic humor he thought to die himself, instantly, to jump off the bridge while still holding on. "That would teach this fool." But he wanted to live and to live life fully.

"What a choice I have to make; how shall I ever decide?"

As time went by, still no one came. The critical moment of decision was drawing near. To show his commitment to his own goals, he would have to continue on his journey now. It was already almost too late to arrive in time. But what a terrible choice to have to make.

A new thought occurred to him. While he could not pull this other up solely by his own efforts, if the other would shorten the rope from his end by curling it around his waist again and again, together they could do it. Actually, the other could do it by himself, so long as he, standing on the bridge, kept it still and steady.

"Now listen," he shouted down. "I think I know how to save you." And he explained his plan. But the other wasn't interested. "You mean you won't help?" "But I told you I cannot pull you up myself, and I don't think I can hang on much longer either."

"You must try," the other shouted back in tears. "If you fail, I die."

The point of decision arrived. What should he do? "My life or this other's?" And then a new idea. A revelation. So new, in fact, it seemed heretical, so alien was it to his traditional way of thinking.

"I want you to listen carefully," he said, "because I mean what I am about to say. I will not accept the position of choice for your life, only for my own; the position of choice for your own life I hereby give back to you."

"What do you mean?" the other asked, afraid.

"I mean, simply, it's up to you. You decide which way this ends. I will become the counterweight. You do the pulling and bring yourself up. I will even tug a little from here." He began unwinding the rope from around his waist and braced himself anew against the side.

"You cannot mean what you say," the other shrieked. "You would not be so selfish. I am your responsibility. What could be so important that you would let someone die? Do not do this to me."

He waited many moments. There was no change in the tension of the rope.

"I accept your choice," he said, at last, and freed his hands.

© *The Bridge—Friedman's Fables by Edwin Friedman / Used by permission.*

UNPACKING THE FABLE

At first read, this fable might appear to be contrary to the message of the Gospel. The laying down of one's life for another is at the very core of Jesus' life and message. We who follow Christ are called to live a life of compassion and sacrifice. Like His parabolic teaching of the *Good Samaritan*, Jesus challenge us not to turn a blind eye to the needs all around us.

But the situation surrounding this fable depicts something different. The storyline of *The Bridge* is not about whether we have the love and compassion required to be willing to hold the rope for another. The issue is one of personal responsibility. Jesus often included a call for personal responsibility during and after he healed others. Some examples include the washing in the pool of Siloam (John 9:7), the call to go and tell, or not tell the religious leaders about what has occurred (Luke 5:12-16), and his calling and the following of the disciples (Luke 22:39-46).

Danish philosopher, Søren Kierkegaard stated:*"There are two ways to be fooled. One is to believe what is not true; The other is to refuse to accept what is true."*[65]

The man who entered the bridge was in pursuit of life and its purposes. The metaphor of being on a road and crossing over a bridge should not be missed. In order to move into a greater understanding of life and its purposes, and to discover one's place and unique contribution, choices related to greater differentiation must be made.

As the story unfolds, the man crossing the bridge is challenged to offer help to another who refuses to take responsibility for his choices. Note the statement made by the one who walked over the bridge and its inclusion of differentiation:

"I will not accept the position of choice for your life, only for my own; the position of choice for your own life I hereby give back to you."

Down through the years, Christ-followers have sometimes become fooled into believing that taking responsibility for other's choices is an act of love. We have wanted to help so badly that we lessen the demands of faith. We have often distorted the Gospel and we have taken away personal responsibility and obedience. When that is done, we have turned those we hope to reach into spectators, not participants.

Choices means change.
Change means taking responsibility.
Taking responsibility results in ownership and growth.

While holding the rope is an act of care and love, taking responsibility for another's choice is not. It is why Jesus himself often asked those who cried out to Him for help, "What do you want?" (Mark 10:46-52, John 1:35-42)

BLAMING OTHERS

The choices made on the bridge illustrate issues related to differentiation, or the lack thereof. One participant makes his choice on the basis of being self-defined, and one does not.

The participant who lacked self-definition and refused to take responsibility for his choices, is a stark picture of those who cast personal responsibility onto others through words of guilt, shame, and personal manipulation.

When the second man was confronted and challenged about his unwillingness to choose, his response reveals how blinding this pattern of behavior can become: *"You cannot mean what you say,"* the other shrieked. *"You would not be so selfish. I am your responsibility. What could be so important that you would let someone die? Do not do this to me."*

It is important to note a couple things.

First, we need to acknowledge that many people in our world do not have a choice. Their plight and genuine needs should not be swept into this fable, or our discussion. Many people have little hope that life will ever improve because of the world and its choices. These are not the subject of Friedman's fable, nor the reason why this story is being used as part of a discussion on transitions.

Secondly, it is important to note that Jesus himself did not grant every request that came to Him. His declaration to the Rich Young Ruler is an example of this (Mark 10:17-31). Jesus presented the choice for the Young Ruler to sell all of his possessions, and when he declined and walked away, Jesus did not chase after him.

The point is that Jesus did not take responsibility for the choices that He asked others to make. Instead, He called those he touched (and is calling us today), to a differentiated life; one of wholeness and health. The message of the Gospel, and the call to surrender to Christ requires that you and I make the choice to respond. It is an act of differentiation. Each of us brings who we are to Christ, taking responsibility for both our need of a Savior, and our response of repentance and future obedience. Salvation is Jesus' exchange of His life for ours, and it involves our choice *leave our nets* and abandon our lives of sin (John 8:11).

SELF-RESPONSIBILITY

The Deciding Transition, and the move from calling to contribution, ushers in the challenge of self-differentiation. It moves each of us closer to accepting and embracing God's unique design for our lives. It is a step closer to being free to be who God has shaped us to be. The individuals who reach the end of their life more in love with and committed to Jesus, have made a choice to grow both in their dependency on Christ and in their self-differentiation.

Our identities often become enmeshed in what we do, as oppose to who we are. We falsely adopt an identity based upon where we work, who we know, and the possessions we own, as oppose to living a life defined as a child of God.

If we don't take steps toward greater self-awareness and differentiation, we often begin to look back to yesterday's success as something that should open the door for today's challenges. We seek security as opposed to obedience, refusing to take risks that move us beyond circumstances we cannot control.

If we don't take steps toward greater self-awareness and differentiation, we end up living a life of entitlement, looking to others to pay the price for life's rewards. We move into patterns of blame, shame and guilt to appease the frustration of not taking responsibility for our own growth.

Parker Palmer, in his book *Let Your Life Speak,* gives us an important final word related to these issues through the lens of self-care:

"Self-care is never a selfish act—it is simply good stewardship of the only gift I have, the gift I was put on earth to offer others. Anytime we can listen to true self and give the care it requires, we do it not only for ourselves, but for the many others whose lives we touch."[66]

God uses the Deciding Transition to dislodge issues of fear, complacency, and plateaued growth by challenging each of us to be who He has shaped us to be. Differentiation is the call to accept who we are, and who we are not, and be willing to more fully embrace God's shaping of our lives. This opens the door to discover our unique and ultimate Kingdom contribution.

Will you choose to live an abundant life with Jesus?

Will you choose to be all of who you are and to share that gift with others?

Will you choose to discover the unique role in the Kingdom that only you can fill?

THINKING IT OVER

You | One-on-One | Coaching | Group

Below is a guide to help you better process what you've just read. It can be used as you review the ideas personally, as a one-on-one discussion tool, as a small group interaction guide, or as a resource for a coaching conversation between you and a personal development coach.

If you are using *Deciding* with a small group, the following provides reflection questions for your <u>eighth</u> (and final) group conversation.

Reflect on the opening quote from Church Swindoll:

"We are all faced with a series of great opportunities brilliantly disguised as impossible situations."

Read Hebrews 11:1-3; 8-12

Reflect on the following questions:

- Past behaviors can sometimes dictate future response. What behavior, or patterns of behavior, do you know you need to change or take more responsibility for in the future?

- What issues have you been avoiding that you now feel God wants you to address?

- In the past, how have you rescued others, instead of empowering them to take responsibility for their own actions? Why did you rescue them?

WANT MORE?

Here is a link to Leader Breakthru's website that will take you further on topics covered in this chapter:

www.leaderbreakthru.com/deciding

PART FOUR

forwarding

One does not surrender a life in an instant.
That which is lifelong can only be surrendered in a lifetime.[67]

—ELISABETH ELLIOT

I have been driven many times upon my knees by the overwhelming
conviction that I had no where else to go. My own wisdom and that of
all about me seemed insufficient for that day.

—ABRAHAM LINCOLN

resourcing contribution

This chapter introduces a series of resources developed by Leader Breakthru to help you go deeper as you process the Deciding Transition. Each resource is available to you as you navigate this important time in your journey.

THE APEX ONLINE PROCESS

Apex is a step-by-step, personal development process that walks you through the Deciding Transition and helps you articulate your unique Kingdom contribution.

During the Apex Process, you review your past and your stewardship of the deposits God has placed into your life. You also seek to integrate your core passions and gifting, which leads you to developing a statement of your Major Role and identifying your Effective Methods. Your final steps are to look at how you want to live in the days ahead, and summarize your work into a one-page, Personal Life Mandate.

Learn more at: leaderbreakthru.com/apex

COACHING

Coaching is all about the person, not just the problem they face. Coaches walk alongside and draw insights out while mentors walk ahead and deposit insights within.

Those who face transitions need a coach to walk alongside them and draw out insights, as well as periodic mentoring that can provide additional insights and clarity.

The benefits of coaching can be summed up in one word: *perspective*. By asking discovery-based questions, coaches help those experiencing the transition better recognize God's shaping work.

The most important contribution a coach can make to those in the Deciding Transition is to help challenge their assumptions and self-limiting beliefs. Everyone can benefit from a coach. Leader Breakthru can help you find a Personal Development Life Coach to help you gain clarity. Don't try to navigate the murky waters of your transition alone.

Learn more at: leaderbreakthru.com/coaching

THE IDEA COACHING PATHWAY

Having a structured path for a coaching conversation can be the difference between a helpful talk and a breakthrough conversation. The *IDEA Coaching Pathway* consists of four stepping-stones that guide an effective coaching conversation. Those steps are: *Identify, Discover, Evaluate* and *Act*.

Identify: The first step is to connect with the person and begin to build rapport and trust. The coachee and the coach identifies the core desire and the most helpful outcome that could be achieved from the conversation.

Discover: The second step down the pathway is exploring the past and circumstances related to the coaching focus through questions and active listening, the challenges are surfaced.

Evaluate: The third step is the discernment of how God might be at work shaping this person through their current circumstances or problem. The goal is to pinpoint the issue that is holding back the desired solution or answer.

Act: The final step is one of action, helping the coachee determine 1-2 strategic, SMART action steps, and then closing the conversation by reviewing their take-away.

COACHING OTHERS

You may already be a coach, or have the gifting to become a coach. Integrating coaching skills with personal development can result in breakthrough for those you coach. Leader Breakthru can train you how to coach the development of Christ-followers. Check out the Coaching Skills Training and Certification Training offered by Leader Breakthru:

Learn more at: leaderbreakthru.com/training/coach-certificate.php

SPIRITUAL DIRECTION

Coaching and Spiritual Direction use many of the same skills. The main difference is that Spiritual Directors focus on interior formation, where coaches offer a wider bandwidth of topics and concerns. Do you want to talk about whether you need a Coach or Spiritual Director? Contact Leader Breakthru and we will help you get the answers you need.

SABBATICAL PLANNING

Vocational ministry leaders need, and benefit from, a regular time of rest and renewal every seven years. A Sabbatical is a time away to renew and refocus life direction and deepen one's walk with Christ. Many leaders have included a sabbatical when they are processing the Deciding Transition. Leader Breakthru offers help in planning your sabbatical, and coaching while you are in the midst of a sabbatical.

100-DAY PLAN

The first one hundred days after any transition is critical. Decision-making and a plan to turn insights into new behavior are an important part of getting all you can out of your transition. Leader Breakthru offers a free resource to help you look at this important period of time in a focused, intentional way.

Learn more at: lbu.leaderbreakthru.com/products/the-100-day-plan/

THE EVERY STRATEGY

One of the common action steps coming out of the Deciding Transition is to become more intentional in one's spiritual disciplines, and making time to be with God. Leader Breakthru has developed a free tool that provides a practical approach to creating more space for God in your busy schedule.

Learn more at: lbu.leaderbreakthru.com/products/the-every-strategy/

a word to leaders

The future is not about slick curriculum, or five easy steps—instead it will be about the presence of Christ permeating the lives and lifestyles of those who love Him. Peter announced the same characteristics as he moved into embracing his contribution:

> *"I have neither silver nor gold, but what I have, I give to you: In the name of Jesus Christ the Nazarene, get up and walk!"* (Acts 3:6)

The Deciding Transition moves a Christ-follower and leader beyond yesterday's renewal, and into the next chapter of life and ministry. There is more to the Christ-like life than just living to sustain an organization or ministry, or acheiving "success" in life. Leaders who are effective in the second-half of life and ministry, and who finish well, live out of a deeper intimacy with Christ, and operate from a different authority base. They move away from ministering only out of a base of relationship, position or expertise, and move into a time of ministering from a base of greater, spiritual authority.

WHAT IS SPIRITUAL AUTHORITY?

In his book, *The Making of a Leader*, Dr. J. Robert Clinton describes spiritual authority as follows:

> *"Spiritual authority is not a goal but rather a by-product. It is a delegated authority that comes from God. Spiritual authority comes out of experience with God. A leader does not seek spiritual authority; a leader seeks to know God. Maturity processing enhances this desire to know God. Spiritual authority results from a leader's experience with God."*[68]

Influence and leadership are issues of authority. Godly leadership is the result of leading from a base of spiritual authority. In the second-half of ministry, effectiveness in ministry flows out of being. The source of one's authority to do ministry no longer is a by-product of natural abilities, youthful passion, zeal, training or degrees. Authority to lead is sourced by the presence of the Triune God who is at work in and through a leader.

- The Father confers on those who have surrendered to Him and His plans an ability to hear His voice, know His desires, and discern His will (John 5:19,20)

- The Son grants His presence and authority to those who are aligned with Him, granting His power to minister based upon a follower's growing trust and dependency (Matthew 28:18-20).

- The Spirit endows that leader with power, increased insight, wisdom, and the ability to discern God's purposes, as He leads and guides those surrendered to Christ into all truth (John 16:13).

Spiritual authority is the by-product of the presence of God working in and through our lives. It is conferred not earned. It is the result of intentional postures or paths taken by a leader that promote greater alignment and dependency on Christ. Each path or posture runs in direct opposition to that which comes "natural" for most leaders. Four intentional postures include:

1. **The Path of Surrender**—This path requires choices about who will reign and rule in the heart of a leader. Surrender stands in direct opposition to our desire to be in control, and our fear of losing direct influence.

2. **The Path of Alignment**—This path requires choices to seek the will and way of the Father over loving our own ways. It is about detaching ourselves from our own plans, our own goals and even our own vision of how life and challenges should go.

3. **The Path of Dependence**—This path requires choices to move beyond our own giftedness, natural abilities and strength, and into deeper levels of trust and reliance on God's Spirit and presence. It is about wanting to follow our love and worship of Christ, as opposed to wanting to be known as a successful leader.

4. **The Path of Humility**—This path requires choices to serve others and to be willing to expose what one does not know, rather than always displaying what one does know. It is also about admitting our need for others more than focusing on their need for us.

In the future, people who follow you into the heat of battle, and into the war being fought over the hearts and lives of people today, are following the presence of Christ in you. They follow those who possess a spiritual authority that has been conferred by Christ.

Paul expressed this core concept in 1 Corinthians 1:12 when he addressed the factions found within the believers in Corinth. "What I mean is this: One of you says, "I follow Paul"; another, "I follow Apollos"; another, "I follow Cephas"; still another, "I follow Christ." All who found themselves embroiled in this divisive battle were challenged to look beyond each leader, and instead, to follow the presence and leadership of Christ.

Leaders, like all Christ-followers, are broken cisterns; vulnerable and ever aware of their shortcomings. Like those who follow them, leaders must courageously align and depend more and more on Christ, to the point of daily sacrifice and surrender. The fragrance of Christ is the result of those behind-the-scenes moments of surrender, which makes all the difference for leadership in the second-half.

Pause for a moment.

Take a few quiet minutes and ask yourself these questions. Reflect on your responses before you move forward:

What is the source of my leadership?

What is the reason that people should follow the leadership that I offer?

How do I know that the ministry (fruit) of my leadership is producing a fruit that remains? (John 15:16)

A PERSONAL STORY

It feels like I (Terry) have spent much of my life trying to learn the truths of this chapter.

For much of my life, I have believed that people want to follow a "dynamic leader." They desire to follow someone who "knows where they are going" and has the answers for the problems of today. In my early years, I read books of successful church and business leaders. I ate up the latest leadership books, and tried many of the approaches of recognized leaders. Most of my time was spent battling the allocation of my time. Would it be time spent with God, or time spent listening to others who were more well known and leading from a greater platform? My daily surrender to the King often took second chair. The tyranny of the urgent became the preoccupation of many of my days.

God moved in on me during my Deciding Transition. He used my own "stuff" to reveal my brokenness that I could no longer ignore. I remember the day I was confronted by the Holy Spirit with the truth of Matthew 3:17.

The relationship that existed between the Father and His Son was declared at the moment of Jesus' Baptism: *"This is my beloved Son in whom I am well pleased."* On that day I finally stopped and took in those words for the first time.

- How could I have missed that these words were spoken to Jesus before the <u>first</u> days of His public ministry?

- How could I have not seen that the Father's love for His Son was already established, and would not change, regardless of the acts He would perform?

- What had caused me to be so blind that those same words that came out of heaven on that day, are the same words that Jesus had said to me the night I had fully surrendered to Him?

I was overwhelmed.

I had wandered around this truth before, but not like this moment. And not with the impact I was experiencing on this day. I began to weep. My tears were out of my deep love for my God, and my deep sorrow from my own unbelief.

I had studied the words of this verse many times before. I had processed these words on a more intellectual level. I am sure that my focus in the past was the launch of Jesus' ministry, and the impact the account had on His time in the wilderness.

But not on that day.

On that day I began to embrace a truth that I had wanted to be true for many years. I had battled to accept Jesus' approval of who I am in my earlier days with Christ. But on this day I finally opened the doors of my life to an invasion of Christ's love that I had yet to experience. Jesus' love for me, and Jesus' acceptance of me, was for me. He was well pleased with me, not because of all I have done, but because of who I am.

This journey still continues.

I still fight to stay within the mindset of ministering more out of whose I am, as opposed to all I offer. I will continue to work out this truth. But the good news is that while this battle will always be on my résumé, I am on the other side of the mountain as it relates to this truth. Something has changed. I have changed. The net result was a new authority to minister. Not as a result of what I know, or the skills I have, but an authority that comes out of His presence and reveals itself in ways unknown to me.

If you find yourself in the Deciding Transition, you can count on being challenged by God to live and lead differently into the future. What has worked for you up to this point may not be the basis of your influence in the days ahead. There is a real possibility that you will be called to places yet unknown. You most likely will be required to lead others who possess greater skills and abilities than you, and who are more educated and experienced than you. You will need to lead differently. You will need to lead out of a greater sense of spiritual authority as opposed to your natural abilities or acquired skills.

To get to this new place:

- You may be challenged to stop hiding behind the wounds of your upbringing and feelings of inadequacy, fear and insecurity.

- You may be challenged to stop excusing your inaction because of a lack of resources, a lack of gifting, or a lack of people to follow you.

- You may also be challenged to move beyond your need for acceptance, recognition, and approval, or the needing to prove, justify or be right.

- As a result of the Deciding Transition, there is a good chance you will be challenged to go to a new place with God.

People may follow you in the future, but why? And to where? Will they follow you because of your skills and abilities? Or will they follow you because they sense a deeper love and devotion to Christ? Answers to these questions are yours to decide.

All the more reason to get all you can out of your Deciding Transition.

notes

[1] M. Craig Barnes, *Sacred Thirst* (Zondervan; Unabridged edition, 2001), p.58

[2] William Bridges, *Transitions: Making the Sense of Life's Changes* (DeCapo Lifelong Books, 4th Edition, 2017) p. 9

[3] Terry B. Walling, *Stuck! Navigating Life and Leadership Transitions* (CreateSpace Publishing Platform, Revised Edition 2015) p.13

[4] Os Guinness, *The Call: Finding and Fulfilling the Central Purpose of Your Life* (Thomas Nelson, 2003) p.32

[5] Janet Hagberg and Robert Guelich, *The Critical Journey: Stages in the Life of Faith* (Sheffield Publishing Company, 2004) p.13

[6] Mike Yacconielli as quoted in *The Blue Book*, Jim Branch (CreateSpace Publishing Platform, 2016) p.118

[7] C.S. Lewis as quoted by Os Guniness in *The Call*, p.97

[8] Josh Packard and Ashleigh Hope, *Church Refugees* (Group Publishing, 2015) Locator 310

[9] Josh Packard and Ashleigh Hope, Locator 177

[10] Christianity Today, The CT Editorial (February 27, 2008)

[11] Os Guinness, p.16 and p.3

[12] Brent Curtis & John Eldredge, *Sacred Romance* (Thomas Nelson Publishers, 1997) p.1

[13] Thomas Merton, *New Seeds of Contemplation* (New Directions; Reprint edition, 2007), p.100

[14] Os Guinness, p.242

[15] C.S. Lewis, *The Chronicles of Narnia: The Silver Chair* (Harper Collins Media Edition, 2010)

[16] Parker Palmer, *A Hidden Wholeness: The Journey Toward an Undivided Life* (Jossey-Bass; 1st edition, 2009), p.39

[17] Brennan Manning, *Ruthless Trust* (Harper Collins Reprint, 2004) p.57

[18] David Brenner, *The Gift of Being Yourself* (IVP Books Expanded Edition, 2015) p.18

[19] Andrew Murrary as quoted in V. Raymond Edman, *They Found the Secret* (Zondervan, 1984) p.88

[20] Raymond V. Edman, p.121

[21] Frederick Buechner, *A Room Called Remember* (HarperOne, 1992), p.14

[22] Archibald Hart, *Adrenaline and Stress* (W. Pub Group, 1995) p.6

[23] Parker Palmer, p.71

[24] Brennan Manning, p.122

[25] Janet Hagberg and Robert Guelich, p.87

[26] Christian History Institute: Module 207—Bernard Clairvaux on Love (www. christianhistoryinstitute. Org/study/module/Bernard)

[27] Christian History Institute: Module 207

[28] Wyatt North: J.R.R Tolkien: *A Life Inspired* (Wyatt North Publishing, 2014) p.31

[29] Bob Bufford, *Halftime Moving from Success to Significance* (Zondervan; Anniversary edition, October 6, 2015)

[30] J. Robert Clinton, *Strategic Concepts* (Barnabas Publishers, 2005) p.37

[31] Greg Cootsona, *Say Yes to No* (Harmony, 2009) p.86

[32] St. Irenaeus of Lyons as quoted by Good Reads

[33] Chuck Swindoll, *Intimacy with the Almighty* (Thomas Nelson, 2000) p.3

[34] Terry B. Walling, *IDEA Coaching Pathway* (CreateSpace Publishing Platform, 2015) pps.19-30

[35] Terry B. Walling, *Stuck!*, p.14

[36] Gordon MacDonald, *A Resilient Life* (Thomas Nelson, 2006) – Amazon Kindle, Locator 1076

[37] Gordon MacDonald, Amazon Kindle, Locator 1078

[38] Tom Patterson, *Living the Life You Were Meant to Live* (Thomas Nelson, 1998) p.85

[39] Martin Luther, *Defense of All the Articles* (1521)-goodreads.com-22880

40 Richard Rhor, *Everything Belongs: The Gift of Contemplative Prayer* (The Crossroads Publishing Company, 2003) p.61

41 Parker Palmer, *Let Your Life Speak: Listening for the Voice of Vocation.* (Jossey-Bass, 1999) p.18

42 Rickard Foster, *Celebration of Discipline: The Path to Spiritual Growth,* (HarperSan Francisco, 1998) p.7

43 Adele Ahlberg Calhoun, *Spiritual Disciplines* (IVP Books, Revised, 2015). p.13

44 Adele Ahlberg Callhoun, p.109

45 Henri Nouwen, *The Way of the Heart* (Ballantine Books Reprint, 2003) pps. 37-38

46 Adele Ahlberg Callhoun, p.13

47 Steven Smith, *Embracing Soul Care* (Kregel Publication, 2006) p.124

48 Chuck Swindoll, p.16

49 John Ortberg, *The Life You've Always Wanted* (Zondervan, 1997) p.79

50 Mark Buchanan, *The Rest of God* (Thomas Nelson, 2007) p.45

51 A.W. Tozer, *The Pursuit of God,* (Christian Publications, 1947) need p.21

52 Greg Frizzell, *Returning to Holiness* (Master Design, 2000) p.72

53 Daniel Henderson, *Old Paths, New Power: Awakening Your Church through Prayer and the Ministry of the Word* (Moody, 2016), p.48

54 A.W. Tozer, p.37

55 Richard Foster, p.118

56 Ken Blanchard and Phil Hodges, *Lead Like Jesus* (Thomas Nelson, 2005) p. 47

57 Kyle Idleman, *The End of Me* (Cook, 2015), p.82

58 Elizabeth Elliott, www.elisabethelliot.org

59 Terry B. Walling, *Stuck!,* p.35

60 Mike Harland, LifeWay Worship, Transformational Church Tour, 2011

61 Paul David Tripp, *New Morning Mercies: A Daily Gospel Devotional* (Crossway, 2014) 1/8/17

62 Edwin H. Friedman, *The Failure of Nerve* (Seabury Books, NewYork, NY), p.14

63 Murray Bowen, *The Self Under Siege: A Therapeutic Model for Differentiation*, p.72

64 Edwin H. Friedman, p.21

65 Søren Kierkegaard as quoted on the blog: Common Sense ethics [http://www.commonsenseethics.com/blog/creating-what-you-dont-want-through-the-law-of-attraction]

66 Parker Palmer, p.30

67 Elizabeth Elliott, www.elisabethelliot.org

68 J. Robert Clinton, *The Making of a Leader* (NavPress, 1988), p.145

Appendix A.
Small Group Guide

A RESOURCE FOR SMALL GROUPS, READING GROUPS OR PEER COACHING GROUPS

At the end of each chapter is a series of reflective questions to help a Christ-follower personally process the insights regarding life transitions. These questions are designed to help an individual glean important insights that can only come from experiencing a transition.

Deciding is also an excellent small group discussion resource. These concepts have been used by book-groups as the basis for reflection and study, and by buddy-read partners who desire to work through the book together.

The Four Major Parts of Deciding

1. **Preparing:** Laying the Foundations (ch. 1-3)

2. **Navigating:** Deciding Narrative & Personal Development Summaries (ch. 4-8)

3. **Interpreting:** Three ways to view the issues of Deciding (ch. 9-11)

4. **Forwarding:** Resources & A Word to Vocational Leaders (ch. 12-13)

TYPICAL SMALL GROUP FORMAT

Week One:

Introduce the book and hear each person's personal story.

For Next Time—Assignment: Read chapters 1-3

Week Two:

Discuss chapters 1-3 / Share Insights about the Deciding Transition

For Next Time—Assignment: Read chapters 4-5

Week Three:

Discuss chapters 4-5 / Entry and Evaluation

For Next Time—Assignment: Read chapters 6-7

Week Four:

Discuss chapters 6-7 / Alignment and Direction

For Next Time—Assignment: Read chapter 8

Week Five:

Discuss chapter 8 / Challenge and Moving Forward

For Next Time—Assignment: Read chapters 9-10

Week Six:

Discuss chapters 9-10 / Postures and Obstacles

For Next Time—Assignment: Read chapters 11-13

Week Seven:

Discuss chapters 11-13 / Differentiation and the Future

For Next Time—Assignment: Summarize your insights from the book

Week Eight:

Summary Discussions / Share insights about the Deciding Transition

The following pages provide an outline for each week of a small group discussion of *Deciding*. It has been designed so that the role of facilitating each meeting can be shared. Each meeting includes an order for the discussion and questions to help guide the discussion.

WEEK ONE—INTRODUCTION AND STORIES

In the first meeting, the group should spend time introducing themselves to one another and the concept of transitions.

Each of us will go through a series of transitions as we journey with Christ. The issue is not whether we will go through transitions, the question is whether our transitions will go through us, and whether we have gained all we can out of our transitions.

Have the group leader for that night reflect on the overall format for the small group, and provide an overview of the book and its various sections.

Together, read pps. 10-14 about how to get the most out of this book.

Next, review the overview of the Deciding Transition on pps. 15-17.

Have the group discuss how they currently see their journey with Christ in light of the description provided.

Spend the remaining time allowing each person to introduce themselves to the group, beginning with the group facilitator.

Have each person reflect on these three questions:

- What are you hoping to gain through this reading/discussion?
- What has been your most significant transition in your past?
- Do you currently feel you are in a time of transition?

Close in prayer asking the Spirit of God to lead and guide the discussion and learning in the future.

Assignment: *Read chapters 1-3*

WEEK TWO—ESSENTIALS OF THE DECIDING TRANSITION

Open the meeting with a time to reconnect and pray.

The purpose of this time is to review some of the core foundations the book highlights as we seek to go deeper in our understanding of the Deciding Transition.

Use the following questions to help the group discuss the contents of chapters 1-3.

Ask the group to share some <u>overall</u> highlights from the three chapters.

- What stood out to you from your reading?

From chapter one, lets discuss the difference between calling and contribution.

- How does the author describe the issue of calling?
- What is his description of contribution?
- What could be an indication that God is moving someone from calling to contribution?

From chapter two, what are your thoughts related to the choices that Deciding Transition often surfaces? Who do you know has experienced the need to choose between the good and the best?

From chapter three, we find this quote: *We live situationally and selectively, but God desires for each of us to live sovereignly.* Let's discuss how that affects our view of how God is shaping our lives, and what each of us needs to begin to see in the bigger picture of our lives.

Allow the group to discuss other thoughts that surfaced from the first three chapters. Is there anything else that stands out to us, and questions these insights might have raised?

Assignment: *Read chapters 4-5 (Note that chapters of 4-8 are written in narrative form, highlighting the Deciding Transition of Rick).*

WEEK THREE—ENTRY AND EVALUATION

Open the meeting with a time to reconnect and pray.

Before launching into the discussion, refer to the *Transition Life Cycle* found on p. 17.

The *Transition Life Cycle* illustrates a generic path that a transition often takes.

Note that each of the next five chapters coincide with the Life Cycle: entry, evaluation, alignment, direction and challenge. This meeting seeks to highlight the entry and evaluation phases of the Deciding Transition.

Ask the group to share some 1-2 <u>overall</u> highlights from the two chapters.

- What stood out to you from the reading for this meeting?

In chapter four, the coaching conversation surfaces that Rick is in a transition.

- What stood out to you related to how the transition began? What was Rick experiencing? How would one know if they are in this transition?

On pps. 52-58 note the issues that surfaced in the midst of Rick's transition. Let's talk about these issues and others that can/do occur when someone faces this in-between time in the mid-game.

Let's review the Burnout Scale on pps. 76-77. What stands out to us as we review the scale? How does the scale impact where each of us might be right now?

Closure: What is the take-away for each of us from our discussion? What was most helpful or what was most insightful from these chapters and our encounter with the first two phases of the Deciding Transition?

Assignment: *Read chapters 6-7 and be prepared to discuss them at our next time together.*

Close in prayer.

WEEK FOUR—ALIGNMENT AND DIRECTION

Open the meeting with a time to reconnect and pray.

Before we head into our discussion tonight, what's standing out to us related to our understanding of the Deciding Transition?

Has anyone who might be in the Deciding Transition received greater clarity or insight from what we have covered thus far in our discussions?

Allow time for open dialog and interaction.

In our time together we now focus on the second-half of the Deciding Transition; the *Alignment* and *Direction Phases.*

Ask the group to share 1-2 <u>overall</u> highlights from the two chapters read.

- What stood out to you from the reading related to *Alignment* and *Direction* phases?

Issues of trust will often surface during the Deciding Transition. In chapter 6, what were your thoughts related to trust? What is the group's reaction to the Trust Helix diagram on p. 86.

During the Back Story from chapter 6, they discuss the idea of "The Wall." What did you understand "The Wall" to be, and how does it relate with your experience?

In chapter seven, God begins to reveal both purpose and direction to Rick. Let's talk about how the direction came, and what other ways God might begin to provide direction and a way forward.

Many of us struggle with saying "no" when needs or opportunities present themselves. Let's review the Back Story section of this chapter and talk about what you found helpful.

The focus of this discussion was direction as it relates to coming out of the Deciding Transition. There may be some of us who long for that to occur, but they have not been able to break through. Who tonight might like prayer for their transition, and the ability to begin to see new direction and answers in the days ahead?

Pray for those who might be requesting prayer.

Close the overall discussion with prayer.

Assignment: *Read chapter 8.*

WEEK FIVE—THE FAITH CHALLENGE

Open the meeting with a time to reconnect and pray

Tonight our discussion focuses on the ending of the Deciding Transition and the call to greater faith and trust.

It is a good time to look back and review together what we've learned about this transition that moves us from discovering our calling to clarifying our unique, Kingdom contribution.

Let's spend a little bit of time going back and remembering how the Deciding Transition occurs. Let's re-read the Back Story from this chapter that discusses how God uses this transition to shape our lives. But first, let's review the life cycle of a transition:

> *Entry: What do we remember about what launches someone into this transition?*
>
> *Evaluation: What surfaced in the work God began to do during this transition?*
>
> *Alignment: How does God pinpoint issues we need to address to move forward?*
>
> *Direction: How do we begin to recognize when the transition is coming to an end?*

Now, let's think back and review the issues that surface related to our development.

> *Two-track Formation: What are the implications of both being & doing?*
>
> *Burnout: How might each of us be susceptible to burnout?*
>
> *The Wall: What are the symptoms of confronting The Wall?*
>
> *Saying No: How can we say no in the future, in order to say yes?*

For the remainder of our time, let's shift our attention now to the faith that is often required to move beyond the time of transition.

Ask the group to share some <u>overall</u> highlights from the chapter that was read.

- What stood out to you related to Faith Challenge?

What stands out as we think about the choices that need to be made as a result of insights gained by Rick from his transition? What type of choices could be part of exiting a transition?

Let's discuss the idea of planning out change and new behavior. How do you react to the idea of a 100-Day Plan? When might it be helpful? When might it not be helpful?

Ask one of the participants to summarize the discussion from the group.

Close the overall discussion with prayer.

Assignment: *Read chapters 11-13*

WEEK SIX—POSTURES AND OBSTACLES

Open the meeting with a time to reconnect and pray.

In this time of discussion, we seek to go after the keys to navigating the Deciding Transition successfully, and the obstacles we could face. It is important to remind ourselves that the Deciding Transition often represents a time when Christ-followers and leaders alike plateau. The challenges become too great, causing them to return back to things they have always done, as opposed to moving onto the new things God has for them to do.

Ask group members to summarize what they saw to be the most important insights from reading the chapters on (1) postures that help to better navigate the transition, and (2) obstacles that often surface as a result of the transition.

Review insights from chapter 9.

Let's discuss the idea of postures. How do you understand what the word "postures" means? What are some postures that you would normally take? What did the chapter offer in terms of new, or different postures from those we would adopt during a time of transition?

Let's talk about this idea of "hearing God's voice." Read as a group, 1 Kings 19:11-13. Notice that Elijah was called to find God's voice; not in the big or the extravagant moments, but as a "still small voice." What does that say related to hearing God during a transition period?

Now let's move the discussion to some of the potential obstacles to recognizing how God is at work. Which of the obstacles felt relevant to you?

- The Anxious

- The Ambitious

- The Angry

- The Automatic

What does the "aligned life" mean? How do we know if we are in alignment with how God is at work in our lives during this transition? What are some of the ways you determine that?

Let's get in groups of 2 and discuss what we're hearing regarding obstacles and how to better align with God. After a time of discussion, pray for one another.

Assignment: *Read chapters 11-13*

WEEK SEVEN—DIFFERENTIATION AND THE FUTURE

Open the meeting with a time to reconnect and pray.

Welcome everyone back, reminding them that next week will be the final week together discussing this book and the issues of the Deciding Transition. Talk over any ideas the group might want to explore in terms of completing the topic (i.e., dinner together, dessert, talking about next book, etc.)

Our reading this week went after a topic that is not often discussed in leadership settings or the church. Differentiation explores how we can better be who God has made us to be, while in context and very much a part of community.

A proper understanding of this concept moves us past issues of in-dependence, or dependence, and onto becoming healthy individuals who seek an inter-dependent relationship with others.

So let's start tonight by going back and reading the fable by Edwin Friedman, called *The Bridge*. Ask for a volunteer to read it for the group. (Read pages 145-149).

Let's begin first by generally processing this fable. What stood out to you? What was the key insight for you as you read the story?

How could this fable be miss-interpreted? What could be some of the issues it surfaces that could be taken too far? Where (if at all) did you feel uncomfortable as you read the story?

What insights did you glean from this fable as it relates to your unique contribution? Does this fable help empower you to say "no" to respon-sibilities that are less that God's best for you?

Note the resources available to help extend the learning and under-standing related to God's shaping work of each of our lives (chapter 12). In particular, highlight the Apex Online process for those who want to go deeper in understanding and clarifying their unique contribution. (leaderbreakthru.com/apex)

Closing: *Next week we will focus on summarizing our insights from the book, and its application to each of our journeys with Christ.*

Between now and our next time together, look back through the book at the things you highlighted from your reading. Bring 2-3 insights you want to take with you into the future.

WEEK EIGHT—SUMMARIZING INSIGHTS

Groups often use a meal or dessert time to close their discussion of the book.

After some informal time together, go around and ask each member to share what stood out to them.

Note: If the group wants to continue, focused on the topic of contribution, introduce the idea of working through the Apex Online Process as a group. Each person registers for the online process, (www.leaderbreakthru.com/apex) and Leader Breakthru offers a Small Group Discussion Guide:

Close the time in prayer, offering thanks for the discussion and insights that have been gained.

Appendix B.
Coach's Guide & Questions

COACHING THE DECIDING TRANSITION USING THIS BOOK

Issue: Clarifying Contribution

Topics: Major Role, Effective Methods, Priorities and Choices

Typical Coaching Series: Six Coaching Appointments / 45 min. each

SESSION 1:
Overview the coachee's core desire and outcome for this coaching.
Read chapters 1-3

SESSION 2:
Overview the coachee's past turning points and insights (review Post-It Note Timeline, if created)
Read chapters 4-5

SESSION 3:
Discuss issues of contribution and the need for deeper intimacy with Christ.
Read chapters 6-7

SESSION 4:
Discuss issues of alignment and the first draft of contribution
Read chapters 8-9

SESSION 5:
Refine contribution: Major Role
Read chapters 10-12

SESSION 6:

Discuss obstacles and challenges as the individual moves beyond the Deciding Transition.

COACHING QUESTIONS: CONTRIBUTION

- If I were to ask someone who knows you well, what would they say is the way you have influenced their life the most?

- Talk about the few things you would love to do more of, or focus on, if you just had more time.

- What do you find yourself saying "yes" to more than you should? What are you not saying "no" to that you know you should?

- How has God worked in the past when you faced a moment that is similar? What typically are some of the things He does to help give you direction? Assurance?

- When others have affirmed that God has used you in their life, what do they say? What are they typically telling you that you do well?

- What choices do you know you need to make in the days ahead to be able to do more of what God has shaped you to do?

- What major roadblocks need to be overcome in order for you to be free to be you in the days ahead?

- What do you have to offer?

- How would you describe your influence to others?

- How does your current work/job let you live out this influence?

- Of all that you do, when do you feel you are most being you?

- What part of your job allows you to live into being you?

- What parts of your job keep you from being you?

- What might need to be enhanced in your job? Adjusted? Changed?

- How do you currently make important decisions?

- How do your core methods help you live out your role?

- What are the interior issues God seems to be addressing? Readdressing?

TRANSITION QUESTIONS: PROCESSING GOD'S SHAPING WORK

Isolation: *When a leader is setting aside of a leader from normal influence/involvement to hear from God.*

- What are you sensing about being connected to the people or events around you?

- What does God seem to be saying/doing when you're alone?

Life Crisis: *When a leader experiences special intense situations of pressure in human experiences that test and teach dependence.*

- Talk to me about the impact of all these recent events on you and your view of things.

- Where (or to whom) do you often go when these types of things happen to you?

Leadership Backlash: *When a leader experiences conflicts in ministry, work, or on a team and gets resistance from followers.*

- As hard as it is to experience people's rejection and hurt, what could this be teaching you about how God can use these moments to forge character?

- What are you sensing it is doing to you and your values or convictions?

Negative Preparation: *When a leader experiences difficult circumstances that dislodge and free them to move on to their next stage of development.*

- How are all of these experiences impacting your overall development as a leader?

- Are their people in your life who have a "big picture" view of your situation? What are they telling you?

Integrity Checks: *A test that God uses to evaluate whether a leader's heart and inner convictions are consistent with their outward actions.*

- Tell me what you think is being tested inside of you right now.

- If you could state in one or two words the core conviction this is touching within you, what would they be?

Obedience Checks: *A test of a leader's capacity to hear from God and to respond through intentional steps or actions in order to align with God's purposes.*

- Tell me what's coming to you out of the Word right now as you reflect on this.

- What's the core action or behavior you believe God is asking you to take?

Word Checks: *A test of a leader's capacity to hear from God and from His Word and to apply revelation to their life and ministry.*

- Tell me what's coming to you out of the Word right now as you reflect on this.

- What's the core action or behavior you believe God is asking you to take?

Divine Contact: *When a leader comes in contact with a key person at a crucial moment that helps ensure future development.*

- Who are the people God uses to speak into your life? Trusted friend? Out of the blue?

- How do they typically get through to you?

- Who has God used the most to speak into your life? What are they saying to you about this situation?

Destiny Experiences: *When a leader hears God speaking/intervening* *with insight concerning future direction and destiny.*

- Tell me about what you sense God was doing/saying by allowing this to happen.

- How does your experience right now line up with the last several months?

Destiny Revelation: *A test of a leader's capacity to hear from God concerning future direction and ultimate destiny.*

- What or how did you realize this was God actually speaking or "connecting the dots?"
- Has this same truth been confirmed in other ways to you?

Destiny Fulfillment: *Moments when God's direction and desires come into existence and the next steps are made clear.*

- Look back and talk to me about how this fits in to your overall life/development.
- Tell me how you see all these things fitting together. What makes it more than just circumstantial?

Faith Challenge: *A test of a leader's willingness to take steps of faith and grow in capacity to trust God.*

- How did you realize that this was God actually speaking to you to step out?
- Has this same truth been confirmed in other ways to you?

the leadership development series

Leader Breakthru's Leadership Development Series consists of three books that take a closer look at the three significant transition moments that every Christ-follower will face. Each of these books can be used as a personal read, a small group resource or as a one-on-one coaching resource. For an introduction to the concept of transitions and an overview of these transitions, check out the book *Stuck! Navigating Life & Leadership Transitions,* by Terry Walling.

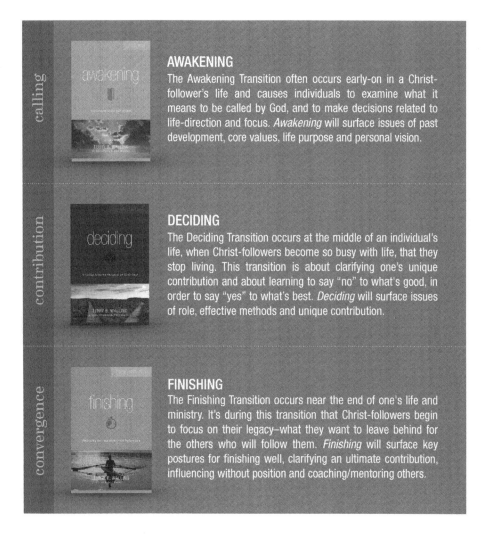

AWAKENING
The Awakening Transition often occurs early-on in a Christ-follower's life and causes individuals to examine what it means to be called by God, and to make decisions related to life-direction and focus. *Awakening* will surface issues of past development, core values, life purpose and personal vision.

DECIDING
The Deciding Transition occurs at the middle of an individual's life, when Christ-followers become so busy with life, that they stop living. This transition is about clarifying one's unique contribution and about learning to say "no" to what's good, in order to say "yes" to what's best. *Deciding* will surface issues of role, effective methods and unique contribution.

FINISHING
The Finishing Transition occurs near the end of one's life and ministry. It's during this transition that Christ-followers begin to focus on their legacy—what they want to leave behind for the others who will follow them. *Finishing* will surface key postures for finishing well, clarifying an ultimate contribution, influencing without position and coaching/mentoring others.

3 Core Processes™

Leader Breakthru offers three core, personal development processes that are designed to guide the on-going development of a Christ-follower. Together they comprise a leadership development system for churches, missions, ministries and organizations.

If you'd like more information about these processes, would like to go through one of the processes online, or would like to gain a license to facilitate one of the processes in your context, please visit: leaderbreakthru.com

calling

FOCUSED LIVING
The Focused Living Process consists of six-sessions related to clarifying life direction and personal calling. This process helps leaders and all Christ-followers gain perspective through the development of core values, a statement of being (life purpose) and a statement of doing (personal vision).

contribution

APEX
The APEX Process consists of eight-sessions that bring greater clarity to a Christ-follower's unique, personal contribution. This process will help individuals discover issues related to their major role and effective methods, and will provide a decision-making grid called a "Personal Life Mandate" that will help to guide any choices that lay ahead.

convergence

RESONANCE
The Resonance Process is a series of three preparatory meetings and three strategic discussions by those who love Christ and desire to finish well. This process helps Christ-followers to clarify how to have influence without position, empower others and leave behind a godly legacy.

92804019R00104

Made in the USA
Columbia, SC
01 April 2018